THE LAYMAN IN THE CHURCH

ABOUT THE BOOK

"Laymen have their rights which the clergy must respect," declared Pope Pius XII at the Second Congress of the Lay Apostolate. One of these rights is that of bearing witness to Christian doctrine and practice. LAYMAN IN THE CHURCH is an eloquent expression of this testimony. It speaks vigorously and clearly of the relation between the laity and the hierarchy, and of the friction that may sometimes develop. In addition to a general discussion of the place of the layman in the structure of the Church, there are treatments of the role of the laity in the Church in America, and of what laymen expect from the Second Vatican Council in the areas of liturgical reform, the theology of the episcopal office, social reform, and adaptation to the needs of the twentieth century.

QUAESTIONES DISPUTATAE

THE LAYMAN
IN THE CHURCH

EDITED BY

JAMES O'GARA

HERDER AND HERDER

1962

HERDER AND HERDER NEW YORK

232 Madison Avenue, New York 16, N. Y.

The chapters of this book originally appeared in "The Commonweal," published by The Commonweal Publishing Co., Inc., New York. The Publishers are very grateful to The Commonweal Publishing Company for permission to collect the articles into book form.

Nihil obstat: Reverend Donald W. Kraus, Ph.D.
Censor Librorum
Imprimatur: Right Reverend Monsignor Vincent M. Leonard
Vicar General, Diocese of Pittsburgh
November 4, 1962

Library of Congress Catalog Card Number: 62-19563

© 1962 The Commonweal Publishing Co., Inc.

Made and printed in the United States of America

CONTENTS

INTRODUCTION

by JAMES O'GARA

Ten years ago this book would hardly have been possible. Ten years from now, it can be hoped, its contents will seem hopelessly dated.

With the exception of the paper by Monsignor John Tracy Ellis, the essays that make up this volume were written in anticipation of the Second Vatican Council. Even before the Council assembles, it has become clear that the very preparation for the great event has itself been a source of hope and vitality for the Church. This preparation has already led to considerable thought on a great many subjects crucial to the Church, including the role of the laity, the subject explored in this collection.

In the months that have intervened between the call of Pope John XXIII and the actual convening of the Ecumenical Council, the laity in many nations have been urged to make known their hopes and aspirations, criticisms and complaints. Perhaps the most specific of these invitations was that of Francis Cardinal Koenig of Vienna, a member of the Central Preparatory Commission for the Council. Speaking at a meeting of Austrian Catholic journalists, Cardinal Koenig said: "Do not wait for the bishop or for a report from Rome, if you have something to say about the Council. Sound a warning whenever you feel that you ought to. Urge, when you feel urging is necessary. . . . Report everything that the people and the Catholics expect concerning the Council."

It was in response to these invitations, and particularly to that of Cardinal Koenig, that these essays were written. If they are frank, it is with the conviction that this is a time when the well-being of the Church demands no less from us than complete openness, complete honesty. If they are sometimes critical in tone, it is with the self-criticism of loyal sons. If they are sometimes impatient, it is with the impatience of those who have glimpsed the true beauty of the Church and who are eager for others to see the same vision. It is in this spirit that these essays were written, and it is only in this spirit that they can profitably be read.

Charles M. Herzfeld suggests in his remarks that our ability to examine our own performance without passion is an indication of growing Catholic maturity. In this he is surely right, and yet it would be foolish to imagine that there will be none to misunderstand the purpose and spirit of this work. The siege mentality is not yet completely dead, and there are those among us who see any effort at self-criticism as giving aid and comfort to enemies of the Church. Such misunderstandings are probably inevitable; nonetheless, we would be failing in our duty if we let fear of them deter us from what needs to be done.

Abbé Eugene Jarry has pointed out that the best of current Catholic theology looks two ways: it strives, first of all, for a closer and more vital contact with our traditions, which means discarding many purely defensive Counter Reformation habits of mind; secondly, this desire to draw nourishment from our traditional roots stems not from any desire to linger romantically in the past but from a determination to move forward, to come to grips with the world in which we find ourselves. The effort to re-define the layman's role in the Church is an essential part of this endeavor.

But such an attempt has to be seen in its proper context. In his introductory essay Father Hovda stresses that we are emerging from a period of intense and unbalanced theological reaction. Historically, we know that the Church necessarily emphasizes now one value, now another, depending on the situation she faces. As Father Hovda notes in his essay, the present position of the layman can properly be understood only in these terms.

There is no doubt that in the Middle Ages, and even before, the clergy performed tasks which were not part of their essential ministry. They did so not because they were hungry for power but because tasks that needed doing would not have been done without their intervention. Education was to a large extent confined to the clergy, and to only a fraction of the clergy at that. For much of the work that required education no one was available but the clergy.

Given this situation, it was inevitable that the role of the layman would become more and more passive. In the late Middle Ages, however, various movements arose which had as their aim the restoration of the layman to his proper place. Here one thinks pre-eminently of the Franciscan movement, which was essentially lay in character and which was, despite the later abuses of the Spiritual Franciscans, truly Catholic.

The welcome such efforts received indicates the hunger people had for a more active role in the Church. Tragically, however, some of these movements were not soundly conceived or well led. They called into question the hiararchical character of the Church; they challenged the divine foundation of the visible Church. Even before the Protestant Reformation, lay rebelliousness and errors of

9

this nature had produced a certain anti-lay reaction among the clergy.

Then, of course, came the Reformation. There is no doubt, I think, that the Reformation owed much of the popular support it attracted to its emphasis on a role for lay piety. When the Reformers spoke about the priesthood of the laity, they were, of course, simply stressing a venerable and respected Catholic teaching — a teaching reaffirmed as recently as this year in a pastoral letter with that very title by the Most Reverend Emile-Joseph de Smedt, Bishop of Bruges, Belgium. But the initiators of the Protestant Reformation were not content to emphasize the traditional Christian teaching on the role of the baptized and confirmed believer. Instead they coupled their appeal to lay piety with an all-out attack on the hierarchical character of the Church and a denial of the divine foundation of the visible Church. The point is crucial, for if the conception of the priesthood of the laity was traditional Catholic teaching, this development was heresy and had to be dealt with as such. The aftermath was as inevitable as anything in history can be said to be.

An attack on the Church which placed great stress on lay participation produced an opposite and extreme reaction inside the Church. The process of clericalization was speeded up, and in many ecclesiastical quarters the laity came to be almost objects of fear. Indeed, to this very day there are people to whom the very phrase, "priesthood of the faithful," has a suspiciously "Protestant" sound to it, as Philip Scharper suggests in his remarks.

What I have done here, of course, is to reduce complex volumes of history to a few sketchy paragraphs. Yet the picture presented is, I think, essentially true, even if lacking much of its complexity. The Church moved from a period in which the clergy were almost the only educated men into one in which the very structure of the Church was under serious and continuing attack. Thesis produced antithesis, in this case an almost exclusive stress on the teaching and governing authority of the hierarchy.

We should be clear on this point. There can be no question of the central role of the hierarchy in the Church. This is beyond dispute. As Joseph E. Cunneen points out, any Catholic who honestly grapples with his temporal vocation in the world comes to see the centrality of the bishop's role. Yet, as Pope Pius XII said, "It would be minimizing the real nature of the Church and her social character to distinguish in her a purely active element, the ecclesiastical authorities, and, on the other hand, a purely passive element, the laymen."

To ignore this point is to run the risk of clericalism. I use the word for lack of a better one, yet I do so with some hesitation, because it has an unpleasant ring to it. I would emphasize, therefore, that I use the term in a purely descriptive rather than a pejorative way, to describe a tendency to see the Church only in terms of priests and bishops and to reduce the laity to a purely passive role.

Because of its central place in the life of the Church, the liturgy is the best example of this danger in practice, as John B. Mannion notes in his contribution. Originally the faithful participated in offering the mysteries, performed in a language they understood. But gradually they became more and more removed, until we came close to the danger of having religion by proxy. The banquet table became a rail of separation, and a semi-private offering of Mass on one side of the rail was accompanied by private devotions on the other. This process reached its ultimate when infrequent Communion became the rule; then the celebrant not only offered Mass

11

but received Communion as a proxy for the congregation. This situation was changed only by St. Pius X, and this not so very many years ago.

Clericalism and lay apathy go hand in hand. The combination does more than alter the basic spirit of the liturgy; it reduces the role of the layman to that of passive bystander in almost every area. While clericalism seems to guard the strength of the Church in the face of attack, it in fact weakens it and reduces the area of the Church's influence.

As many scholars have noted, an excessively clerical attitude detracts from an eschatological vision of history. This is so because we can have a real awareness of Christian history only if we have a highly developed sense of ourselves as God's holy people and of the Church as a community called to a collective vocation. When this is lacking, the layman has no sense of Christian vocation. His role is then reduced to little more than keeping a tidy set of rules, contributing to the support of his pastor and staying out of ecclesiastical affairs.

The problem is not that the clergy have an inordinate sense of power. This formulation would be a vulgarization and distortion of the issue. What is involved is a question of emphasis, of an approach which cannot help but reduce the role of the layman, from that of serving on the frontier where Church and world meet to that of being spectator and dues-payer. When that happens, the Church does not and cannot permeate the environment.

This, I take it, is what William J. Nagle means when he says that laymen have failed in their work of bringing Christ into the world, and this, I submit, is precisely our present situation, for the Church today is absent from entire areas of arts and letters, industry and culture, politics and intellectual life. The gap between secular and Christian life is large and growing; indeed, in much of modern life, de-Christianization is not a threat but a fact.

This is the situation the modern Popes have confronted. Looking out from St. Peter's in Rome, they beheld a Christendom turned in on itself and afraid, while outside the modern world was being born, to a large extent with values hostile to the Church. It seems clear that the central effort of the modern Popes from Leo XIII onward has been directed to meeting this challenge.

Social reform, ecumenicism, the lay apostolate, the liturgical movement, Biblical studies — all look to our roots in the past, in order to deal more effectively with the present. Any one of these major concerns of the modern Popes would require a separate essay to begin to do it justice, and on the question of the layman's role alone citations of Papal exhortations could be multiplied almost indefinitely, from the time of Pope Leo in 1890 to that of Pope John XXIII today. Perhaps this by Pope Pius XII in 1946 may be taken to represent the spirit and direction of all: "The laity must above all have a conviction ever more and more exact, not only of belonging to the Church, but of *being* the Church, that is to say, the community of the faithful on earth under the leadership of the common head, the Pope, and the bishops in communion with him. They are the Church."

Response to papal calls for increased lay participation was, I think, heartfelt and enthusiastic, indicating something of the love of the layman for the Church and of his desire to serve. As Monsignor Ellis says, when the history of these years is written, there will be few more striking notes than the emergence of the laity. In the period between the two World Wars, in particular, hopes ran very high indeed, as zealous priests and laymen tried to translate the papal calls for action into reality. And yet today one cannot escape the impression that there has developed a certain confusion of purpose, a certain lessening of enthusiasm.

In a different context in his essay Justus George Lawler writes that we are moving into the second stage of the modern Church, in which the achievements of the post-Vatican and post-Modernist period will be coordinated, sheared of extravagances and given new energy. It might be argued that some such change is all that is involved here, in what at first glance appears to be a slackening of energy. Nonetheless, I am myself convinced that all is not well and that more is involved than any inevitable loss of the perhaps too enthusiastic early hopes.

It is to this problem that Daniel Callahan addresses himself. Given the present juridical and canonical status of the layman in the Church, he writes, it is exceedingly difficult to see how either lay aspirations or clerical desires for a more integrated laity can be realized. And this, it seems to me, remains in the end the crux of the question we confront.

This is not to say that more could not be done than has yet been attempted. Indeed, it is hard to understand why more has not been done, given the urgency of the situation and the fervor of papal admonitions, and in this sense clerical complacency and lay apathy continue to be our most immediate and pressing problems. But it remains true that it is far easier to say what the layman's role is *not* than to describe what it is, and in the long run it is hard to quarrel with the thesis that the layman's role does require more exact formulation than it has yet received. This is a task of considerable magnitude and extreme delicacy, and for its accomplishment we must, of necessity, look to the Pope and the bishops in Council. It is to this end that these essays were written and this volume published.

14

I

THE CATHOLIC LAYMAN IN AMERICA TODAY

John Tracy Ellis

Each age in the long and eventful life of the Church has its distinguishing characteristics. When the history of this second half of the twentieth century is written there will, in all probability, be few more striking notes than the emergence of the laity into a strong and active role as collaborators with the clergy in the apostolate. So marked has been this development that there has even emerged a theology of the lay movement, a new tract, as it were, which theologians have been refining in recent years in a way that suggests the revival of the part once played in the early Church by the deacon who assisted the priests and bishops in advancing the word of God through the ancient pagan world.

In part this expanding concept of the layman's place in the divine economy of salvation is an answer to a need. For every well-informed Catholic has for some time been aware that the rate of increase of the faithful — to say nothing of the increase of potential converts among our separated brethren — has become so rapid that the supply of priests and religious for their spiritual care can in no way keep pace, with the result that the emphasis on the need for lay apostles is by no means confined to Latin America but has become virtually worldwide.

In fact, with the exception of certain favored areas like the

Republic of Ireland and the Archdiocese of Boston in our own country, lay Catholics — or non-Catholics who may offer a prospect of conversion — far outdistance the proportional growth of priestly and religious vocations. That is one reason why our generation, more than any other in modern times, has heard so insistent a call for lay assistance and participation in the work of the Church.

In recognition of this central fact of contemporary Catholicism there was convened in 1951 the first World Congress of the Lay Apostolate, which was followed six years later by a second World Congress at Rome in October, 1957. To both of these gatherings Pope Pius XII delivered memorable addresses which outlined the respective roles that the clergy and the laity were expected to play in furthering the apostolate so that it might embrace men of every continent, of every color, and of every race.

On both occasions the Pontiff made clear the necessary distinctions between the function of the clergy, particularly the bishops, who alone represent the teaching authority of the Church, and that of the laity who are asked to cooperate with those in ecclesiastical authority. But Pius XII was at pains to emphasize the layman's share, stating that — to quote the words he used in 1951 — "the assistance rendered by the laity to the apostolate is an indispensable necessity."

Six years later the Holy Father returned to the same theme, delineating once more as precisely as possible the apostolic functions of the priest and of the layman. And in this latter address to the second World Congress Pius XII maintained that the value and efficacy of the apostolate exercised by any participant was dependent not on his rank but on what the Pope called "his personal ability and supernatural gifts." Lay teachers, religious, missionary catechists, and all to whom the Church entrusted the

16

truths of faith he said, "can properly apply to themselves the Lord's words: 'You are the salt of the earth,' and 'You are the light of the world.'"

In view of this development in world Catholicism, what, one may ask, is the situation in which the Catholic laity of the United States find themselves, and how does that situation fit them to offer the maximum response to the responsibilities which the Holy See has asked them to assume?

First, they constitute a body of nearly forty-three million souls joined by a deep supernatural faith and an abiding love for Christ's Church that makes them one of the world's most promising reservoirs of Catholic strength and renewal. Theirs is a faith with historic roots that reach back to the Spanish pioneers who brought Catholicism to Florida, the Southwest, and California before the United States itself was born; a faith that was practiced by the French in the Mississippi Valley and the region of the Great Lakes when what we know as the Middle West was still largely an untracked wilderness; a faith for which the tiny minority of their English Catholic forebears in colonial Maryland and Pennsylvania suffered ostracism and legal proscription.

In other words, the impressive Catholic laity of today must not be thought a new thing on the American scene; they are rather the product of between three hundred and four hundred years of growth in the soil of this Republic. Secondly, this laity — thanks to God's bountiful providence and to the frugal living and dedicated labor of their ancestors and of themselves — are the wealthiest group of Catholics in the world, and thus in a material and external sense their numbers and their wealth constitute them the strongest laity within the universal Church.

More important, however, than numbers and wealth has been

17

the intellectual advance of the Catholics of the United States. It is a feature that gains strength with each passing year as thousands of young Americans stream forth from the colleges and universities of the land intellectually equipped to occupy an articulate and meaningful place in national life. With this heightened intellectual and cultural prestige, with the deepening knowledge that accompanies a superior education, there has inevitably appeared a closer scrutiny of all that pertains to the Church, a sharper and more critical turn of mind which makes the educated Catholic layman of this second half of the twentieth century a quite different person from his unlettered immigrant grandparents of two or three generations ago.

Here, then, is a new factor in the Catholicism of our day, a factor that is bound to assume increasing importance in the years ahead, a factor that has, indeed, already had a major share in accelerating the speed at which the Catholic Church of this country has come of age. With this new factor there has come in some sectors of the Catholic community a note of strain in clerical-lay relations.

Here I would wish to emphasize that I have in mind situations quite apart from the indefensible conduct of an insignificant minority of lay Catholics in New Orleans who have gained national notoriety by their defiance of the racial integration policies of their Archbishop. I refer rather to the educated and loyal layman, conscious of the improved position he occupies over that of his grandparents and conscious, too, of the emphasis that the Holy See has repeatedly given of late to the need for the laity to take a more active share in the Church's life and work. It is this type of Catholic layman — devout, fundamentally respectful of authority, alert, and highly trained — who is seeking to find a channel through which he may contribute his talents and special skills to the apostolate of his time.

In that connection I am reminded of a remark made by John Lancaster Spalding, Bishop of Peoria, in 1889 in a letter to William J. Onahan, at the time probably Chicago's most outstanding Catholic layman — a remark quoted by Father David F. Sweeney, O.F.M., in his life of Bishop Spalding. Speaking of the Catholic lay congress being planned for the autumn of that year, Bishop Spalding was intent that there should be some practical results, and in instancing lay cooperation with the clergy he strongly urged that Onahan should, as he said, "devise some means by which laymen may really take part in Church work. . . . Let us cease," said the Bishop, "to pretend to wish to do what we have no intention of doing."

It would be untrue to say that there has been no progress in that respect since Bishop Spalding wrote seventy-three years ago. But it would be less than honest to represent the channels of lay participation in the Church's varied apostolate as fully open to their zeal. Thus James O'Gara of The Commonweal wrote not long ago of the deep conviction that many laymen had concerning the principles of the Papal encyclicals. But, he said, when the layman tries to implement his conviction by doing something about it, he "is frequently rebuffed." He then declared: "All too often, he is made to feel like a stranger where he should be most welcome, in his own parish. This seems to me a major problem, and one I think should be faced more squarely. Until it is, I am afraid lay participation will remain more pious wish than actual fact."

It is, indeed, a major problem, and with the writer's rather lugubrious conclusion I feel compelled to agree. Too many laymen trying to find their place in apostolic action have experienced embarrassing encounters with a certain type of churchman who seems never to have heard Pius XII's exhortation to the clerical delegates of the first World Congress of the Lay Apostolate when he said: 'let them encourage them (the laity), suggesting enterprises to them and welcoming with good will the enterprises which they suggest, approving them in a broadminded way according to their opportuneness. In decisive battles, it is often at the front that the most useful initiatives arise."

More than a century has passed since Orestes Brownson, the best-known Catholic layman of his day, reminded the readers of his *Quarterly Review* that theirs was an age when education and intelligence were not confined to the clergy, and that the grounds of controversy between the Church and its enemies were not exclusively theological, but such as would ultimately be decided by reason rather than authority. In these circumstances, said Brownson, in October of 1860, "the fullest liberty must be given to laymen, compatible with the supremacy of the spiritual order and the discipline of the Church."

If that could be said with warrant in 1860, with how much more cogency do the changed conditions of our day permit it to be said in 1962. Obviously, care must be taken in the layman's execution of his apostolic mandate so that what he says and what he does may not transgress the limits imposed upon him by Catholic doctrine and that he may not find himself at cross purposes with what the Catholic sense would interpret as the legitimate exercise of authority by his ecclesiastical superiors. But by the same token the continued harmony and good order of the Catholic community make it imperative that the clergy be persuaded that present conditions call for a relaxing of some of the power and authority they have been accustomed to exercise over the laity in matters not directly pertaining to their divine mission; that they share, in other words, with the laymen in those areas of the Church's life where the latter's special training and competence entitle them to participate actively in fulfillment of the directives of the Holy See.

Fortunately, the Catholic Church in this country has never been handicapped by the devastating tradition of anticlericalism that has proved so detrimental to religion in much of western Europe and of Latin America. Once only in our history have the relations of clergy and laity undergone a real crisis, when at the close of the eighteenth century there arose the movement known as lay trusteeism which continued to plague certain sections of the American Church as late as the Civil War. It was a costly experience for which a rebellious minority of the laity and a small but defiant and ambitious group of priests were equally to blame. But thanks to the fundamental loyalty of the vast majority of the laity, and of the docile and zealous character of most of the clergy, by the mid-century the worst evils of lay trusteeism had run their course.

Meanwhile, between the hundreds of thousands of incoming immigrants — most of whom were poor, illiterate, and without guidance in a strange land — and the priests who either accompanied them or whom they found on their arrival, there were forged the strongest bonds of affection and mutual esteem as they joined hands to establish their religious life — often in a hostile environment — as well as to insure their material welfare by mutual assistance. The result was the emergence of a relationship between the two ranks that earned the admiration of the Catholic world, a model that has endured to our own day and that is still, thank God, essentially intact.

Yet it would be a disservice to the Church that we love were we to deny the presence in our midst of symptoms that suggest an anticlerical sentiment hitherto unknown to American Catholics. In its issue of April 16 of this year, *America* noted this phenomenon in an editorial that made somber reading for those whose knowledge of history recalled the price that the Church paid in Europe and Latin America during the nineteenth century because of the deadly poison of anticlericalism. Up to the present we have been mercifully spared from this virus, and it is a matter of prime importance for the wholesome Catholic life we have known in the United States that we continue to be kept free from its lethal influence.

If I were asked to suggest the most effective weapons with which to combat anticlericalism, I should be inclined to answer as follows. First, the exercise by both clergy and laity of extreme sensitivity and forbearance in their relations with each other so that nothing be said or done that may exasperate or give cause for needless irritation or offense. And in this category principal emphasis should be placed, I think, on public statements that by the harshness of their tone or the lack of sympathy that they breathe, are likely to wound the feelings of others.

Secondly, there should be a steady and deliberate opening up of new channels for apostolic action to the layman, such as has taken place, for example, in the archdiocese of Montreal where the entire school board has been given over to laymen and in the diocese of Providence where seven out of eleven members of the diocesan school board are laymen. For when one pauses to consider it, could there be any more appropriate arena wherein to implement the layman's apostolic zeal than membership on the board that frames the policies and directs the destinies of the schools that his children attend?

Another important area is the Family Life Apostolate where, I am reliably informed, at least one hundred thousand married couples at the present time are engaged in giving lectures, conducting conferences, writing articles and books, appearing on television and radio programs, participating in neighborhood and community activities in their role as Catholic husbands and wives, and in some dioceses even acting as marriage counsellors.

Thirdly, I think of the Catholic press as an area which, it seems to me, is peculiarly fitted for the laymen and where a number of lay journalists have clearly proven that they not only can conduct a Catholic newspaper with high satisfaction but, perhaps, can do it better than the priest by reason of their technical training and the total dedication that they can bring to the task which the priest is denied because of his simultaneous commitment to other responsibilities.

And last, but by no means the least, are the varied good works of the National Council of Catholic Men and the National Council of Catholic Women which for approximately forty years have been doing yeoman work in activating the laity to a more intelligent and organized service to the Catholic cause. These aspects of the life of the modern Church, then, the diocesan school board, the Family Life Apostolate, and the Catholic press, and the two National Councils have already given proof in certain dioceses that they hold the key for the layman who wishes to function actively in the Church, and that in a way that redounds not only to the advancement of the Catholic apostolate, but as well to the layman's personal honor and distinction.

That the percentage of highly educated and specially trained laymen in the American Church will increase is certain; that this fact will create a more exacting and searching spirit among the laity concerning what they find in the Church is equally certain.

23

It thus behooves all of us, clergy and laity alike, to see to it that the infinitely precious tradition of intimate and warm clerical-lay relations that we of this generation have inherited from the American Catholic past is preserved and passed on to those who come after us.

At times this task will demand patience and forbearance on the part of each of us, but the ultimate good to be served is more than worth the effort, for in the greater participation of the laity in the Church's works lies in part the solution for many of the problems of a harassed and under-staffed clerical body, and in the new avenues opened to lay activity will there be afforded the means for increasing and strengthening the Catholic laymen of the United States along the lines that John Henry Newman had in mind when toward the close of his famous 1851 "Lectures on the Present Position of Catholics in England" he said this:

"What I desiderate in Catholics is the gift of bringing out what their religion is; it is one of these 'better gifts,' of which the Apostle bids you be 'zealous.' You must not hide your talent in a napkin, or your light under a bushel. I want a laity, not arrogant, not rash in speech, not disputatious, but men who know their religon, who enter into it, who know just where they stand, who know what they hold, and what they do not, who know their creed so well, that they can give an account of it, who know so much of history that they can defend it. . . . I have no apprehension you will be the worse Catholics for familiarity with these subjects, provided you cherish a vivid sense of God above and keep in mind that you have souls to be judged and to be saved."

II

THE LAYMAN: VICTIM OF REACTION?

Robert W. Hovda

Reaction is potentially as dangerous a phenomenon as it is natural in every human society, in all movements of human thought and action. Opposition to mistakes or errors, in a philosophy, in a political theory, in an economic program, often finds it difficult to avoid caricaturing its genuine insights and its truth. Reaction constantly threatens to distort truth by losing the balance required for its accurate formulation.

It is impossible to talk about present healthy developments in the theology of the Church, and particularly in the theology of the layman in the Church, without first recognizing that we are emerging from a period of intense and unbalanced theological reaction. We are emerging from a period in which, though the laypeople's part, office, functions, or ministry in the Church was never denied in principle, it was rarely affirmed. The Church's doctrine, however, has never forgotten that, while her worship is hierarchically ordered for the sake of unity, it is the worship of the whole community in which the "amen" is as essential as the Collect.

The Church's doctrine has never forgotten that, while she is structured by the apostolic college of Jesus' institution, she is also the community of the Spirit. The Church's doctrine has never forgotten that while the hierarchical authority rules, it does not rule in a vacuum, without consulting with and listening to the voices of the laypeople, whose sacramental initiation and Christian life render ridiculous the notion of a merely passive laity. The Church's doctrine has never forgotten that, while the hierarchy judges, this very fact demands initiatives from the community, and that sometimes it is the younger member who speaks with greater wisdom.

What movement in the Church would have succeeded, what contemplative or charitable work would have been founded, without this freedom (and responsibility) to create and invent, to suggest, to be heard and to be tested? The saints are a constant witness in the Church's life to these initiatives, to this breathing of the Spirit.

Tradition in the Church is a reality and force with unhappy as well as happy aspects. So many "traditions," purely human customs, habits, attitudes, hide under the cloak of the Gospel truth, of the Good News, which Tradition is bound to bring to men. It is so easy to fail to make the necessary distinctions and to inherit, instead of the freedom offered by God's Word, a kind of slavery to our Christian ancestors. But one of the happy aspects of Tradition's power is the fact that it conserves through periods of ignorance or indifference truths upon which later generations can build, when the ignorance and the indifference have passed.

Thanks to Scripture scholarship, theological exploration, patristic studies, liturgical science, archeology, and church history, we are rediscovering some of these riches of Tradition. Most of us are aware of a transformation, unfortunately just beginning in many places, affecting Catholic public worship, particularly the celebration of the Mass. From inert, if dutiful, worshipers at a rite insufficiently intelligible to them and from which their active participation is almost inevitably excluded, the laity are in some places again becoming listening, praying, singing, sacrificing, communing participants in a living, popular worship which sacrifices nothing of the Church's liturgical wisdom and tradition.

They are also in many places being recalled to their proper ministry and witness in the temporal order, as well as in the Church's missionary evangelization. Who could fail to note the effect on the laity of America of the birth and growth of hundreds of forms, structures, organizations of the lay apostolate, of "Catholic Action," of lay missionary activity? In the liturgical revival and in the lay apostolate we have obvious and convincing evidence of the laity's reintegration in the amazingly clericalized Church of modern times.

But there are other areas where our progress is less obvious. The term "church government" is inadequate because, though the Church is a visible society, a people, it is much more. And no treatment of its life and governance which examines it only as a religious counterpart to political society can be anything but misleading.

The Church is generically different, vastly different, from any human society or institution, including the state. Hence, as Father John Courtney Murray has pointed out, the folly of attempting to argue from the government of the state to the government of the Church, or vice versa. One is human and natural, founded on the social nature of man, formed by the work of human reason, guided by human political wisdom, concerning itself with public order and the external acts of men. The other is divine and supernatural, constituted by the Savior, receiving its basic structure as a gift, with the internal bond of union in the Spirit.

So the Catholic finds no difficulty in the fact that the Church is not a democracy in the political sense. She is Christ's Mystical Body and her transcendent claims make this arrangement indeed impossible. But if she is not a democracy in the political sense, neither is she an autocracy in the political sense, nor a monarchy in the political sense. These categories have no meaning for her. She belongs to another order.

Yet in this "space-between," in this period of the Church in the world, it is not only a worshiping community, not only a community whose task and privilege it is to bear witness to a Word from God. Because it is visible, made up of men, it is also a community with government. The bishops of the apostolic college, gathered around the Roman primacy, are rulers as well as priests and teachers.

If the layman is more than simply one of the "governed," in the political sense, if he has more than a merely passive role to play in this area of the Church's life, it must appear in his relation to the bishop. Does he have any voice in choosing men for the hierarchical ministry? And what power has his voice with the bishop once elected?

The early practice of the Church reveals a definite participation of the laity in the election of bishops. This participation has taken different forms: sometimes the approval (unanimity was apparently sought as a sign of the Spirit's presence) of the nominee of the apostolic college; sometimes the election of several candidates from whom the apostolic college would choose one; sometimes the choice of one of several presented by the apostolic college.

Gradually, however, the voice of the faithful in elections was practically reduced to the voice of kings and princes. Because of this "representative" system and because ecclesiastical offices were at times plums of temporal power and fortune, medieval times saw a practical abandonment of lay consultation in these matters. But the principle remains.

What about the layman's relationship to the bishop once elected? And to the pastor once appointed? How does or should the layman figure in the daily decisions of the Church on many levels and in its legislation? Such decisions concern a multitude of problems, ranging from building programs and methods and measures in the apostolate to questions of church positions on matters of public policy which touch faith and morals. The bishop always functions as the bishop of a Christian community. And the relationship between bishop and the rest of the community is in the Church not only a political relationship. If it were, we could follow the same rules, base our thinking on the same principles, and achieve the same evolution as we have in political life. But the relationship of bishop and people is an organic thing. The Spirit is given to the whole Church. Infallibility belongs to the whole Church. So the bishop exercises his power of ruling and teaching and presiding at public worship in close touch with the whole Church, with the feelings, thoughts, desires of the faithful.

The Church is not only a priestly and institutional reality, she is a prophetical one as well. There is, perhaps there should be, a tension between its priestly and its prophetical missions. In the visible organs of its magisterium, it has the means from Christ of presiding over and directing the members of the Mystical Body. And to the same Church has been given the Spirit Who breathes where He wills. It is death to Christianity when one consents to choose between these elements. Both must be affirmed.

We don't have to consider here what we regard as the Protestant problem. The Reformers made a choice. They chose a prophetical principle divorced from the priestly. The Catholic Church has never made such a choice. She has always affirmed the simultaneous necessity of priesthood and prophecy, of institution and Spirit, of organization and organism.

But if the Catholic Church has not made the choice of the Protestant Reformers, if she has not allowed herself to be forced into that kind of either-or dilemma, we should be less than honest if we did not admit that Protestant and pre-Protestant emphasis on the prophetic has received so reactionary a response from us that we have tended in practice to reduce the Church to the priestly and the institutional. In practice, not in doctrine, I would emphasize. But practice teaches, too, sometimes more powerfully.

Hence freedom of thought and speech and criticism, public opinion, the responsibility of laity and clergy to express their ideas —outside the Church these are almost universally thought to be alien to Catholicism. And within the Church, among most of us, one notices a marked hesitancy to be open, to be forthright, to be critical. As a result of this, a caricature of the Church is almost everywhere today accepted as its authentic portrait. It sees the Church as a mother whose smothering embrace crushes breath and life out of her children, reducing them to a kind of dazed and inert half-human existence.

This reluctance to speak our minds on issues, this irrational kind of "obedience," this assumption that a constructive contribution is an act of disloyalty—this is treason to the Church, to our sacramental initiation, to our bishops and Pope who deserve this contribution, and to the Holy Spirit. It is possible we might make mistakes. This is the risk of life. And judgment is the task of that hierarchical structure which, with the Eucharist it celebrates, is our bond of union. Mistakes are bad only if we are not faithful enough to accept judgment. But there have to be developments, there has to be thinking, there has to be an expression of views, if there is to be anything to judge.

In his essay, "Free Speech in the Church," Father Karl Rahner has strongly affirmed the necessity of an articulate public opinion for the life and health of the Church. Pope Pius XII did the same in his 1950 speech to the International Congress of the Catholic Press, an appeal echoed in the synodal statutes of the Archdiocese of Cologne in 1954. As Father Rahner points out, if the Church is to communicate the good news, the hierarchy in its official teaching capacity must know not only the Message but also the state of the listener, the times in which he lives, his concerns, his mentality, his problems and interests.

Such contributions of public opinion, such criticisms, are acts of love, of a love which penetrates deeply into the meaning of the Church. A true love, based on true knowledge — not the pseudo-love which has to pretend conformity because it is mixed with a kind of servile fear of the hierarchy, or because our own comfort reacts against the prospect of change, or because we really believe the supernatural faith is a gift which relieves us of the necessity of thought. Father Guardini's classic statement is relevant: "Imperfection belongs to the very essence of the Church on earth. This presupposes that we have the courage to endure a permanent state of dissatisfaction."

Somehow we Catholics must reaffirm the prophetic mission (and the priestly) of all members of the Church in practice as we have always maintained it in doctrine. Somehow we must balance the excessive attention we have given to its hierarchical structure (under pressure of controversy) with some advertence to the Church as the community of the faithful. This is difficult to do, because we not only have to train the Church's members to what

31

is for all practical purposes a new concept of responsibility and obedience, but we also have to provide some kind of structures for consultation and for the expression of public opinion. Some bishops have experimented with such structures. Some are meeting with lay advisory councils composed of representatives of the parishes in their dioceses. Some have called meetings of laymen to make suggestions relative to the forthcoming Ecumenical Council. Many have at least some means of occasional contact with already established diocesan lay organizations. There will have to be a good deal of experimentation, no doubt, before any particular system of representation gains widespread acceptance.

Parishes, too, can certainly experiment with various forms of lay councils to meet with the pastor at regular intervals. It is also within the realm of possibility that the Vatican may internationalize itself and avail itself and its congregations of lay opinion through appropriate offices and contacts with lay organizations.

Not that we have no instrumentalities within the Church at present for this intramural dialogue and for these initiatives. We always have, of course, the possibility of personal contact with our pastors and our bishop. We have a Catholic press which is willing, at least in many areas, to voice the opinions of the faithful. There is still great scope for personal initiatives of many kinds within the present structure of parish and diocesan life. We could not have produced great lay figures and great lay periodicals if this were not true.

But the fact that the prophetic voice exists in the same house with the priestly is not enough. There must be some cross-fertilization. There must be some recognition of each by the other. And, in any case, the examples we can think of are rare flowers. The common, garden varieties are mostly under bushels. And they need new structures, as well as a bit of warmth, to tempt them out. It might be added also that our present lay organizations in the Church quite generally feel a need for more autonomy, more trust and confidence, more freedom, if their function is to be really profitable to Catholic life.

In the course of these remarks I have discussed chiefly the layman's contribution of thought, of his temporal competence and experience, of whatever inspirations the Spirit may grant him, in areas of the Church's life which might be described as peripheral. But I did not mean to imply that such contributions are to be restricted to problems of policy, of missionary technique, of an understanding of the times to which the Church addresses herself. I mentioned briefly the liturgical revival, certainly central in the life of the Mystical Body, and the general apostolate of Christian witness.

The recent republication of Cardinal Newman's essay, "On Consulting the Faithful in Matters of Doctrine," reminds us of the layman's part in the development of doctrine, in the Church's growth in its understanding of God's Word. Newman shows the relationship between the magisterium and the faithful in this doctrinal area. Not in terms of an active and a passive element, but a much more complicated relationship — as between a husband and wife in marriage.

What the layman actually believes, particularly when there is a recognizable consensus of faith in the Christian community, is of concern to the whole Church. Newman calls such a consensus: "a testimony of apostolic dogma; a sort of instinct deep in the bosom of the Mystical Body; a direction of the Holy Spirit; an answer to the prayer of the Church; a jealousy of error, which it at once feels as a scandal."

33

It is obvious that this involves heavy responsibilities which many a layman is not eager to assume. He can make this contribution only if he is living the life of the Church at its deepest level of sacramental life, prayer and witness . . . and only if he is fully *lay*. That is, only if he is fully committed as a man or woman and as a Christian to the temporal order, to the secular achievements of his age, to its thought, its culture, its significant movements.

These paragraphs just skim the surface. Much more must be said and discussed and meditated about these problems. One does not say these things to become popular with the laity. And one does not say them as a nihilist or even as a griper. One says them because, when they are forgotten, the Church suffers, not an essential change, but a distortion, a weakening of her native powers, a diminishment of her catholicity, an obscuring of her relevance. Yet she cannot afford to suffer distortion, disease and diminishment in these days when the world is finally prepared to appreciate that idea of the catholic unity of mankind which the Church has carried in her heart as a kind of unrequited love all these centuries.

III

RENEWAL OF THE CHURCH

Philip Scharper

What every Catholic would hope for from the Council is that it succeed in realizing one of the major goals which Pope John set in convoking it: a renewal of the Church which will be so effective that the Church herself will become, by what she is, the most compelling argument for Christian unity.

But it would be a mistake to assume that such reform and renewal were important only to enable the Church to present a fairer face to our separated brothers. On point after point such reform is urgently needed to make the Catholic himself understand the Church more deeply, love her more devotedly, and live in her life more fully.

In what follows, I shall try to set forth what points of renewal seem to me most urgent. They may reflect a parochialism of experience and poverty of observation; but they have also whatever value may attach itself to the reflections of one who has no position to maintain and no interests to serve, except those of Christ in His Church.

First, I would hope that the Council might render more meaningful the statement of Pope Pius XII that this is the Age of the Laity; that the lay person is not only in the front lines of the Church, but "is the Church." A particularly hopeful line of development would seem, to me at least, to lie in exploring the dimensions of the recovered phrase, "the priesthood of the laity." Pius XII declared that lay members of the Church should be informed of their priesthood, and the fact of their priesthood "should neither be minimized nor denied."

These are clear words and strong directives, yet in the years since Pope Pius uttered them I have not heard a single sermon on the priesthood of the laity, been aware of a single study group undertaking it as a subject of inquiry, nor read a single article about it in journals which reach the layman as a matter of policy.

Further, I would hope that any attention given to the role of the laity would allow sociological perspectives in addition to the theological and canonical bases on which the subject must rest.

To cite but an obvious instance: I have known a score of lay editors of Catholic newspapers and magazines, and dozens of dedicated lay teachers in Catholic schools and colleges. These people are not members of the Church in any minimal sense; they are passionately interested in the Church. It is their abiding — often their central — concern. Their home is an *ecclesiola*; their leisure reading has a generous quota of theology — dogmatic, speculative and ascetical; their leisure activities embrace some form of intelligent Catholic Action, and they are concerned with such things as the liturgy and the social teachings of the Church.

Sociologically, in short, they are closer to the ideal of the priesthood than is that consecrated priest who does little serious reading, whose leisure activities, though innocent, are worldly and hence trivial, and whose thinking on social issues reflects the mass media rather than the mind of the Church.

Such a sociological situation does not, of course, affect the theological and canonical status of either priest or lay person, but it obviously cannot (or should not) be brushed aside if one is considering how the lay person is to share in the unfulfilled work of Christ, the High Priest. It means — among many other things that could be cited — that the lay person should have a voice in *some* of the councils within the Church The lay faculty in our schools should be given a larger role in decision-taking and policy-making than is presently the case in many institutions. Further, every effort should be made to treat the layman as though he were in status, as he is in fact, a peer of the priest and religious in the Church's educational mission.

Parishioners could well be consulted about many matters in the parish, such as the best times for weekday Masses and the hearing of confessions, what subjects they wish to hear treated in sermons, and whether or not the preacher can be heard in any case. Indeed, if one could propose it without seeming facetious, a new Canon might call for a Suggestion Box next to the holy water font at the entrance to each church.

These specific examples may well be as banal as I think they are bathetic, but they point to a fact which is neither: the layman is increasingly urged to ponder and fulfill his role in the Church; lay people are increasingly competent to discharge that role, yet are frustrated by the fact that the administrative structures of the Church often make it difficult, if not impossible, for the layman to respond to the very challenges given him by pulpit and press.

Such, at least, was my feeling some months ago when I read in the Catholic press an injunction of Mr. Martin Work, executive director of the National Council of Catholic Men. Mr. Work chided the laity of the United States for not making known to the proper authorities its desires and wishes concerning the forthcoming Council. But no indication was given as to who these authorities were, how they were to be contacted in this case, nor how the public opinon he called for was effectively to be ascertained and presented. I have the greatest respect for Mr. Work, but that is irrelevant here. What is relevant is that another responsibility was being set before the laity, but no provision was made for the discharge of that responsibility. In effect, the lay person was invited to give a broadcast, was ushered into a studio, and then was seated before a dead microphone. He can be pardoned if, at times, he feels like a Kafka-esque creation.

I would also hope that the Council might address itself to the theology of religious toleration and the closely connected question of the relation of Church and State. I am aware, of course, that these questions are — and have long been — in a state of dialectical tension, but there is much in the modern world to suggest that the tension, if long protracted, will be sterile rather than fruitful. There would seem to be as ample theological warrant for the so-called liberal view as there is for the so-called conservative one, and I suspect that on this point "consulting the faithful" of the world would indicate that most of them have long accepted the "liberal" view. For in our times the experience of Northern Europe and North America gives as valid a reading of the mind of the Church as does the history of Southern Europe and South America, and the present vitality of the Northern churches suggests that the Church is most free to be herself when she is as free from privilege as she is from persecution.

Further, the Church's concern with Asia and Africa makes imperative some reasonably definite solution, for here the Church is confronted, not with the religious pluralism of Western experience, but with the pluralism of Protestant, Catholic, Orthodox, Jew, Moslem, Buddhist, Shintoist, *et al.* To confront such traditions with a truncated theology of tolerance or an insistence upon Church-State relations predicated upon an increasingly anachronistic Western historical experience would be in great part to foreclose the future of the Church within these cultures and to force Christ to speak to these peoples, as it were, in a harsh and alien tongue.

Lastly, one would hope that the Council might somehow serve to create a climate of urgency in which theologians would work to discover the practical corollaries of the Church's teachings. We have, for example, recovered, after centuries of virtual ignorance, an awareness of the Church as the Mystical Body of Christ. But theologians, teachers and preachers have, for the most part, seemingly rested in a continually deepening exposition of the doctrine itself, without too much concern for what we might call the practical consequences of the doctrine for those problems which press most heavily upon modern man.

One of those problems is obviously that of race. Surely the doctrine of the Mystical Body has tremendous implications here, but those implications have all too often been glossed over in favor of purely social, political and economic considerations.

One must not judge the past unfairly and must, above all, not blame an earlier generation for lacking insights only painfully gained in our own. Nevertheless, some questions still seem pertinent. Why, for example, were so many Catholic churches in our South segregated so completely for so long a time? What cast of mind accounted for the fact that the Supreme Court decision of 1954 opened the doors of Catholic colleges to more Negroes than had the fact that the Catholic Negro was a member of Christ's Body? How can we still partake of the Eucharist, the Sacrament of Unity, and tranquilly permit Christ, in His Negro and Puerto

Rican brothers, to be confined to slums scarcely fit for even animal occupancy?

Modern man is also vexed by the problem of work. Does it have a meaning beyond the obvious economic one? Can it have a deeper meaning for most workers in a complex, industrialized society where work, it has been alleged, increasingly dehumanizes the worker as man increasingly serves his machines? The problem, of course, is old; only its intensity is new.

The doctrine of the Mystical Body would seem to have implications for at least a partial solution to this problem. It would seem to contain generous hints toward a genuine theology of work which would redeem from meaninglessness the working hours of the Christian's day. The problem is old, but even the phrase, "a theology of work," is relatively new, and the theology itself has scarcely been attempted on a serious scale. I would almost venture the guess that, in the last five years, more theological attention has been paid to the morality of boxing and careless driving than to the development of a theology of work.

Modern man also confronts the new and perplexing problem of international responsibility. One of the cruellest features of the problem is that it catches man at the intersecting point of a declining nationalism in the West and the rising nationalism of the emergent nations of Africa and Asia.

How does the Christian confront this problem? Should he have a sense of guilt at realizing that the "new nations" suffered much from the colonizers of Christian Europe; that very often the Christion missionizing activity was based on charity toward the "natives," but seemed unaware of the prior demands of justice, permitting the exploitation of natural resources while proclaiming the Kingdom of God?

Even if the past were blameless, what, if any, is the Christian's responsibility toward the peoples struggling upward toward a condition of authentic humanity? What response can he make to their often blind but blessed thrust toward freedom from the serfdoms of the past?

Here, too, the doctrine of the Mystical Body would seem to have relevance, but the relevance has yet to be spelled out so often and in such detail that the Catholic cannot evade it. One sees an occasional editorial in the Catholic press on the subject, but rarely one that carries the thought deeper than last year's editorial. Articles on the subject are yet more rare, and books are almost nonexistent. Birth control, yes. Divorce, yes. Population explosion (in relation to birth control), yes. Federal funds for Catholic schools, yes. These subjects are abundantly treated. But why the comparative silence on our responsibilities to the new world which is taking shape before our eyes?

Race, work, international responsibility — three problems which roil the modern world and lacerate the soul of twentieth-century man. But we have come into the twentieth century without an adequate "theology" of race, without an adequate "theology" of work, without an adequate "theology" of international responsibility. We have, in short, come into the twentieth century at the great risk of seeming almost irrelevant in the eyes of the non-Catholic world.

The peril of seeming irrelevance confronts, of course, not only Roman Catholicism but all of the Christian churches equally. In itself, this peril constitutes one of the strongest arguments for Christian unity, and makes it clear that no matter how remote may be unity in creed, unity in charity and concern can suffer no delay. This, I take it, was prominently in the mind of Pope John when

41

he said, in speaking of the Council: "We do not intend to conduct a trial of the past; we do not want to prove who was right or who was wrong. The blame is on both sides. All we want is to say: 'Let us come together. Let us make an end of our divisions.'"

Appeal for unity is, of course, not enough. There must be persuasion as well, and the only reason for writing these lines is that they mirror what one Catholic feels to be involved in one of the announced main purposes of the Council: so to renew the Church that she becomes herself the most persuasive argument for unity, as she stands before the world — not as we Catholics have made her by our pride and folly, our apathy, our hardness of heart, our confusion of national interests and cultural constructs with the essence of the Church — but as she is in the design of Christ: the splendid City on the mountain, its walls and towers constantly aglow as they faithfully reflect the Light of the Sun.

IV

REALITIES OF PARISH LIFE

JOSEPH E. CUNNEEN

Let me strike a sour note at the outset, and suggest that the invitation for laymen to speak out on the coming Council first be considered in the dominant context of Catholic indifference and skepticism. It is true, of course, that in the last few years alumnae groups who wanted to be *au courant* have scheduled at least one speaker who could flavor his talk with words like "ecumenical" and "dialogue," but any idea that the Council requires an involvement and commitment of the entire Church could hardly make much headway against our perennial absorption in building drives and rhetorical anti-Communism. To all outward appearances, the parish clergy and church-going laity possess a united response: the Council is a good idea, but no concern of ours.

And as for consulting laymen, what possibly can Cardinal Koenig, who voiced the explicit invitation, mean? Doubtless there are available amiable eccentrics who specialize in Byzantine liturgies or the history of canon law, but what response outside of downright hilarity would greet any wide-eyed "Catholic Action-ist" who told the local Holy Name Society — to say nothing of that more representative group, the men who do not attend the meetings — that their views on the coming Council were being solicited? "I can't get through to my pastor," one might say, "on why I object to using envelopes in the collection, or why I want to keep my family together, and not ship the kids off to a separate children's Mass; how can I have anything to say to theologians and cardinals?"

Only, of course, no one says this to his bishop; and, unless conditions are very different in Austria, no one says this to Cardinal Koenig, either. A laudable reverence for his role as heir of the Apostles shields him from the vulgarity in which the layman might express his instinctive, somewhat cynical conviction that the business of the Church is an affair for specialists. Occasionally, a dissident voice may reach his ears, but it is apt to sound like what it probably is: a gripe, a clash of personalities, some uninformed and irresponsible petulance. Yet even such expressions have their importance, and partly because of their inadequacy. If we had a strong and continuing tradition of lay responsibility, the voices would be more positive, more confident — and more deeply Christian.

Those who rightly complain of lay immaturity today should be forced to reflect on those patterns in Catholic life which help to prolong indefinitely a state of adolescence. Catholic schools that pride themselves on their discipline rarely provide the most exemplary models of student self-government. Similarly, laymen are often given the impression by their priest friends that any display of initiative will only make their superiors suspicious. One ultimately begins to believe that the atmosphere of ecclesiastical restraint, coupled with a prudence not exclusively spiritual in character, is hardly an ideal one to help the bishop become truly informed about the problems in his diocese.

It would appear, then, that the opening of lines of regular communication within the Church should be an underlying concern throughout the work of the Council. At the same time, it is only just to recognize that gestures of encouragement such as that of Cardinal Koenig are increasingly common on all levels, from the Vatican to the local parish.

The two World Congresses of the Lay Apostolate held at Rome (another is planned for 1963), the first African meeting of the Lay Apostolate at Uganda (1953) and the first Asian meeting at Manila (1955) are important events in the twentieth-century history of the Church. Such international movements as the Y.C.W., Pax Romana, Pax Christi, etc. — some of which seem surprisingly feeble or non-existent in the United States — are playing an indispensable role in world opinion.

When a document on "Temporal Commitment" was recently published by the French Episcopal Commission on Labor, it was the fruit of a collaboration between those bishops who were members of the commitee and the national leaders of the Labor section of Catholic Action. As the preface states, these lay leaders contributed "their experience of the workers' world, their direct observation, which has made it possible for them to see how the worker looks at this commitment." A similar direction is suggested in the proposal of Father Lombardi for the creation of various councils, some composed of laymen, others of both priests and laymen, which would be capped by a lay "Senate of humanity."

Nevertheless, despite the responsible and genuine nature of such appeals, in the day-to-day life of the local church one can easily get the impression that "the age of the layman" is merely a new slogan for the inevitable Catholic organizations, summoned into being to suggest the outlines of vast popular support. Even at the World Lay Congress in Rome, John Todd's report on the first meeting — written for *Downside Review,* Spring 1952 — suggests

45

that genuine communication with authority was short-circuited, and that lay recommendations and resolutions were drastically edited by zealous monsignori. Does the nature of the Church really call for a clerical Sherman Adams, shielding bishops or the Pope from disturbing facts, especially if they are not couched in the terms of seminary rhetoric?

It would be a mockery of any notion of lay responsibility to summon a group into existence that would either never act, or whose judgments—in their own area of competence—were always identical with those of the hierarchy. In a given case, a Catholic labor group might decide to support a strike led by leftist leaders, or involving employees at Catholic institutions. They must not represent the bishop's position unfairly, and should keep in mind that their own is not infallible; nevertheless, I cannot see why they should not abide by their judgment. Another Catholic group, specialists on international affairs, may conclude that America should abandon its policy of trying to exclude Communist China from membership in the United Nations. But will they issue this statement if they know episcopal support will be immediately withdrawn, and their organization accused of indifference to the plight of the "Church of silence"? If they refrain, will their Christianity be more adult? Does the avoidance of embarrassment constitute a victory for the Church?

What is needed, then, it would seem, is not more "study days" on the role of the layman, but a change in attitude which for some may appear to be fundamental. There is no reason, however, to believe that attitudes cannot be changed in the Church if there is a will to dramatize the new approach: consider the revolution accomplished in the half-century since Pius X brought Communion to young children, and began to make us all see the necessity for more frequent reception of the Eucharist. Proposals already made in regard to the Council, advocating greater decentralization and further encouraging lay participation in the liturgy, suggest exciting possibilities.

Would smaller parishes, whose unpretentious structures would use the most economical materials possible, make it easier for all of us to see the altar as central? Studies of modern urbanism by sociologists of religion tend to suggest ecclesiastical units small enough for priests and people to know each other more easily, and in which spontaneous and meaningful ways of using lay assistants might develop naturally. The parish must keep in focus its central activity of celebrating the Christian mysteries, and through this means forming the minds and hearts of Christian adults; Christian parents, especially in these times of revolution, must be so trained that they can assume the major burden for the religious education of their children. This will free the parish to rediscover the essentially missionary dimension of Christianity, and to be present, without righteousness or proselytizing zeal, among the needs and concerns of the total community.

There need be no fear that the layman, in a burst of willful impatience, is straining at the teaching authority of the Church. Any Catholic who honestly grapples with his temporal vocation in the world comes to see the centrality of the bishop's role, and prays only to encounter him more frequently as teacher than as super-administrator. Few are the Sunday sermons which center on doctrine; fewer still are those which help us see in what way doctrines change anything in our lives. In this connection it might be helpful to take seriously Canon Jacques Leclercq's notion of moral heresy, especially since those teachings which are related to the

Christian concept of fraternity are of central concern to every-day life.

We all make too little effort today to see the meaning of Christian poverty; is it an anachronism in our affluent societies of the West? It is hard for us to realize that justice *demands* that we seriously attack the problem of the shocking disparity of living standards between ourselves and the newer nations. Similarly, the same Catholic who is eager to make a personal sacrifice in his contribution to the parochial school in a growing suburban area is rarely helped to realize that his effort to build up Christ's body in his neighborhood is a fraud if it cooperates, even by passive collusion, with a pattern of systematic segregation in the new housing projects which are developing.

No critique could be more telling than Canon Leclercq's summary: "The Catholic, as he is generally conceived, is characterized by his religious practices: he goes to Mass, he goes without meat on Friday; he is not characterized by charity. But this is practice; let us put the question from the doctrinal point of view: the Catholic then is one who *believes* that he must go to Mass and that he must do without meat on Friday, who recognizes that he is at fault if he does not do this; he is not one who *believes* that he must love his neighbor *as* Christ loved us and who acknowledges himself to be at fault if he does not love him *in that manner*."

An informed Catholic can see the importance of such a Council proposal as re-emphasis of the office of bishop, especially since the notion of papal infallibility is usually seen in hopelessly unbalanced perspective. Nevertheless, the layman is apt to fear that the appreciation of such fundamentals will be obscured if the image of the Church projected is one with apparently no decisive and healing word to offer a desperately troubled world on such questions as modern warfare, the limits of nationalism, world hunger and capital punishment.

The Council's concern for our Orthodox brothers is a reason for hope, since among the positive results of the meetings is apt to be warmer and more frequent personal contact, as well as increased mature study of Orthodoxy, perhaps even as part of regular seminary training. Reputable Catholic theologians have often told us that we will be better able to see that which is purely local, transient or unbalanced in our Western Christendom as we gain greater familiarity with the Christian traditions of the East, with its experimental emphasis, its sense of transcendence allied to "negative theology," centered in the mystery of the Holy Trinity.

Unless this new knowledge is merely to be fitted into the rational, positive and technical character of Latin theology, however, must there not be a constant care, whether in the seminary, the pulpit, or the Catholic school, to stress the openness, the continuous operation of every Christian's attempt to appropriate the meaning of Revelation in his lived experience? Will this not lead logically to another of Cardinal Koenig's suggested topics, reforms in canon law pertaining to the reading of "prohibited books"? When there is less emphasis on prohibition, and more on the limited character of infallibility, the merely probable nature of many propositions now often presented as part of Catholic tradition will become clearer, as well as the inevitably speculative character of the bulk of the theological enterprise.

The *magisterium* has always one sure, but rarely employed, way to remind laymen of their vanity and ignorance: ask them to be saints. If we are hard on our pastors, it may finally be because they ask us only to be *regular in our religious practices*. What is crucial for us at the Council is not the precise wording of a decree but a significant reminder that through the Church we are being invited by Christ to share His life.

What is needed at the Council, then, is not better public relations, spectacular demonstrations or an ingenious use of popular jargon. What we must seek is a deeper understanding that the spirit in which the entire Church is called into Council is not for a certain number of days over in Rome, but something to be continued in human contacts and open communication every day in every parish.

V

FIRST, THE LITURGY

John B. Mannion

Of all the actions likely to be taken by the forthcoming Ecumenical Council, few will affect the Catholic people so directly and personally as the liturgical reforms. For most of us, our principal public contact with the Church is Sunday Mass. And indeed, this is as it should be, for the liturgy is "the chief duty and supreme dignity" of Christians, and takes precedence over any other religious activity — public or private, individual or corporate. For this reason the Mass should be our most meaningful Christian experience. That this is not the case is one of the several motives which have prompted the liturgical reforms of recent decades. Pope Pius XI's "outsiders and mute spectators" of 1928 have become Pope John's "telegraph poles" of 1960.

Clearly the reforms instituted have not been adequate to the task of conveying to the people the true nature of liturgical worship and their role in it. Perhaps this is because the changes have been within the structure of the Roman liturgy as it was frozen in the sixteenth century.

To the man of the twentieth century, the Mass does not appear to be what it actually is: a formal proclamation of the Word of God, a sacrificial oblation re-presenting "in mystery" the redemptive work of Christ, and a community meal renewing the covenant

— the pledge of eternal life and love — between the Father and His chosen sons. This threefold reality is not immediately and directly revealed by the words and actions of the Latin rite Mass, which fact has led to a growing realization of the need for further reform.

But why reform? Why not better education in the liturgy as it is? The answer lies in the very essence of what liturgy is. Let us define it here as that complex of rites or sacred signs which contain what they signify and through which God is glorified and man sanctified. No one questions the essential efficacy of the Latin liturgy in glorifying God and sanctifying man. What is in question is its efficacy as "sign," for insofar as our Mass today fails to signify or communicate to the man of today what it actually is, it fails as "sign." A sign which means little or nothing to me is not really a sign at all; it is an enigma.

What we may hope for, then, is that the fathers of the Second Vatican Council will provide us with a complexus of intelligible, meaningful signs (if the reader will forgive the redundant adjectives). Precisely what changes are called for are well known to anyone who has been observing or engaging in the liturgical movement. The innumerable details need not concern us here; those seeking them are earnestly referred to such recent works as H. A. Reinhold's *Bringing the Mass to the People* (Helicon, 1960). Let us be satisfied with selective comments on the broad outline of reforms, keeping in mind that these suggestions are not the official proposals of the Liturgical Conference or any other body; at the same time, insofar as they reflect the writer's study and discussion with clergy and laity, scholars and "typical parishioners," they may be considered representative of a general trend of thought in the Church today.

Taking the Mass in its sequence, it seems imperative that the readings from Scripture should be presented in a manner which clearly demonstrates that this is the formal proclamation, by the Church, of God's revealed Word to His people duly assembled. This might be accomplished by providing that the lessons be read facing the people, from lecterns or ambos (which would also serve the purpose of distinguishing between the "service of the Word" and the service of the altar).

The cycle of selections from the Bible might be expanded, say to three years, so that more of the Word could be offered the people than is now possible in a one-year cycle. Should not more Old Testament readings be included, perhaps by more frequent use of three lessons in the Mass instead of two? And, needless to say, all such readings should be in the language of the people (more on this later), and delivered reverently, not hurriedly for the sake of satisfying an obligation. The ancient "prayer of the faithful" or litany of special intentions might be restored to use to conclude the first important segment of our worship service.

The offertory can easily be revised to make it clearer that the gifts come from the people. At the same time, care should be taken that the offertory rite does not seem to be anything more than a simple presentation of the materials of the sacrifice; the celebrant's prayers at this time seem to make more of it by confusing the offering of the bread and wine with the sacrifice of Christ's Body and Blood.

Some consideration should be given to the prayers and actions of the Canon: why the Preface of the Holy Trinity as the standard Sunday preface? Why invoke Roman saints unknown to us? Why not give more prominence to the concluding elevation and doxology, not delaying the people's response by the celebrant's genuflection or coupling it with the Our Father before Communion? And since the Canon is *the* central action of the Mass, why should it not be celebrated aloud as the focus of our attention?

The relationship between Communion and the sacrificial act might be more evident if the two were not separated by so much time. Couldn't the private prayers of the celebrant be eliminated? And shouldn't it be stressed again that sharing the Eucharistic Food is the proper and normal conclusion of the Mass for all who are present? It would also help if more force were given to the urging of recent Popes that the people receive Hosts consecrated at the same Mass.

The "last Gospel" — like the prayers at the foot of the altar — began as a private devotion of the celebrant, not as prayer proper to public worship. There is considerable opinion that both practices might best be dropped for the sake of clarity.

Among all these changes, however, the central problem remains that of language. If it is a valid principle that changes are intended to make the forms of the liturgy conform more appropriately to their inner nature and purpose and to make them more meaningful to the people, then we cannot lightly dismiss the increasing desire for more vernacular in the rites of our public worship. Since the liturgy is a sacred sign — an external, intelligible signification of an interior, invisible reality — and since words are essential in the sacramental rites, the use of an unknown language obstructs the purpose of liturgy considered as a sign, a means of communication.

Pope John's recent Apostolic Constitution, *Veterum Sapientia,* reaffirms a centuries-old tradition that Latin is the official language of the Western Church. This precise, succinct tongue is admirably suited as the vehicle for preserving normative formulations of Church doctrine, against which all vernacular teaching can be

judged. It serves an equally valuable purpose as the language of
official communications and documents within the universal
Church, and of the official books of the sacred liturgy (Missal,
Office, Ritual, Pontificale, etc.).

This principle would not be compromised if the Church were to
permit vernacular usage in parochial liturgy. It would still be the
Latin rite. The Latin texts would be the norm for all vernacular
editions. Some parts of the Mass might well be retained — without
any threat to intelligibility — in Latin (and Hebrew and Greek),
e.g., the familiar greetings and other versicles, and in prayers said
silently by the priest. Moreover, the liturgy would be celebrated
completely in Latin in monasteries and other religous institutions,
in Rome, perhaps in cathedral churches and at international
gatherings.

To ask that Christians, when assembled in their parish churches,
be permitted to worship in their own language is not to abuse the
honored place of Latin; it is simply to recognize the fact that the
people no longer understand that venerable tongue. Viewed objectively, the loss of Latin as the language of public worship is indeed
a loss, but the same objectivity should tell us that we risk an even
greater loss if we sacrifice meaningful, sincere worship in favor of
this or any other matter of liturgical discipline.

These remarks on the vernacular constitute no attempt to exhaust
the question. But they are deemed necessary, if only because so
many have been led to believe that *Veterum Sapientia* was intended to banish the possibility of vernacular in the liturgy—which
it was not or it would have said so — as well as to stifle any and all
discussion of this possibility — which it was not or it would not
have singled out only those who are "moved by an inordinate
desire for novelty." If not all, then certainly the majority, of those

clergy and laity who call for the vernacular speak from the conviction that they seek only the essential purposes of the Church: the glory of God and the sanctification of man.

The fact that the cry for the vernacular is so widespread among clergy and laity in so many countries (if a vote were feasible, or in order, I would not doubt the outcome) might suggest that the Holy Spirit is active in this matter, again making His inspiration known through the consensus of the faithful. Certainly the fathers of the Council, no matter what their personal preference might be, will consider this a possibility.

Space prohibits any detailed discussion of additional reforms, but a few deserve mention:

It is commonly said that the Divine Office in its present form is not in harmony with the daily routine of the secular clergy in the modern world. Most commentators on the subject urge that the number of "hours" be reduced, that it be recited in the vernacular, that the choral elements be altered for individual use, and that some of the contents be revised.

Lay people would surely benefit if some form of the Office were made available to them — at least as morning and evening prayer, for use individually, in family life, and as a public service in the parish church. In this way, the entire church — not the clergy alone — could share in that prayer which sanctifies the various periods of the day and offers a continuing round of praise to the Father.

At the present time, the Holy See reserves to itself all rights concerning the ordering of the sacred liturgy. It would achieve great pastoral good if the principle of local adaptation were restored by the council. This would allow local ordinaries or the bishops of a country to make adjustments and additions to the liturgy to accommodate local customs and cultures. Consider, for instance, the diverse wedding or funeral customs among such countries as Japan and South Africa, Poland and Indochina, the United States and India. In our own country the local adaptation principle would be more than justified if it resulted in evening Masses regularly, meaningful services for funerals, betrothals, Thanksgiving Day and other American customs, and — most urgently — for wakes, which are uncomfortably empty and un-Christian.

These are but samples of the sort of reforms hoped for among clergy and laity. Unfortunately, they have been articulated publicly only by scholars or specialists, and in books and journals which do not grace every home and rectory library. If our bishops are to engage in the deliberations of the Council with full knowledge of the mind of the faithful, more clergy and laity must speak up.

Such expression of hopes and needs for reform will surely be accepted as a manifestation of genuine concern for the effectiveness of the Church's mission. Let us hope that no false notion of prudence or false concept of the liturgy as the exclusive province of the clergy will restrain lay people from revealing their legitimate and prayerfully considered aspirations concerning liturgical reform. Informed discussion, conducted with charity, loyalty, and mutual respect, can lead to that ordering of the sacred liturgy which permits intelligent and meaningful engagement in the redemptive realities through which we, united to Christ in the unity of the Holy Spirit, offer all honor and glory to the Father.

VI

OUR WASTED INTELLECTUALS

Charles M. Herzfeld

These are exciting times in the life of the Church in America, because there are clear indications that the Church is approaching full maturity. The best evidence of this is the mounting ability of the Catholic community to examine its performance and position calmly and objectively and, beyond this, to invite outside criticism and to listen to it with care. It is now possible, perhaps, as it has not been in the past, to draw attention to an important and difficult problem, namely the relation of the laity and the clergy. In one sense there is no such problem: the Church is One and Indivisible. Yet, in another, more mundane, sense the problem has always existed and always will. The entrance into maturity just noted makes it especially important and fruitful to examine some aspects of this question.

It is no longer adequate to discuss this subject simply in terms of the led and the leaders, because we know that the health of the Church depends to a large degree on the creative and stimulating interaction of laity and clergy. In fact, one might well speak of a need for dialogue between laity and clergy, but this term has become an over-worked cliché, and appeal to it has become an easy way to avoid the hard problems. Yet the notion of dialogue suggests to us that we proceed in a spirit of loving and honest examination of whatever issues arise, and that we remain as free from excessive rhetoric as possible. Only love of the Church can motivate an exploration such as this.

The relation of laity and clergy develops as the Church does. Every generation must create its own relationship, and it must try to go beyond the past in understanding, in effectiveness, and in dedication. Laity and clergy interact in the Church in innumerable ways and on many levels — spiritual, intellectual, sociological, economic, and so on. I would like to explore here a very special segment of the overall problem, restricted to the interaction of a small, though distinctive, part of the laity with the clergy, and examine only a few ways of interacting. The group I wish to consider has no name and is not easy to describe. It consists of all who are creatively involved with ideas and with public issues, such as scholars, teachers, scientists, writers and artists, perceptive administrators, leaders in public service. These people are sometimes called "intellectuals" (though rarely by themselves).

In addition, I limit my remarks to those whose formative years came during or after the depression of the thirties, for it is this younger group which faces most acutely the problems to be discussed. (Parenthetically, it is important to note that many members of the clergy are "creatively involved," and from this aspect operate as "lay" persons.)

My basic proposition is this: The relations of the members of this idea and public issue group with the clergy (and hierarchy) are either non-existent, or else (with some exceptions) completely unsatisfactory.

Let me state at the outset that I believe both sides are at fault in the present situation. Further, the problem must be raised now, because it is one of the most important facing the Church in

America today, and because, I am convinced, the current atmosphere is sufficiently calm that the chances for contributing constructive criticism on the subject are reasonably good. The problem is crucial because it is precisely from this alienated group that the intellectual and cultural leadership in the Church must come, and it is through this group that the Church must largely speak to the rest of society. If, therefore, this group and the clergy "talk past each other" rather than with each other, we are faced with a problem of the utmost seriousness.

We must improve our understanding of the relation of laity and clergy in many areas, but there are three crucial ones. These are, first, lay competence and responsibility; second, the quality of some contributions to the life of the Church made by the clergy; and last, the potentialities and difficulties of creative interaction between laity and clergy.

Let us look first at the matter of lay competence and responsibility. To do so properly, one must be quite clear that we are in no sense discussing matters of faith and doctrine, but only such questions which lie either in scientific, scholarly and artistic fields, or else in areas of prudential judgment of practices and habits. Such questions are not decidable by decree; they are "discussable," and should be discussed more freely.

Unfortunately, the fact of lay competence in these matters is not adequately recognized in practice today. This is so in part because of the popularity of a number of mistaken notions. First, it is assumed that any activity called "Catholic" engages the whole Church. Second, it is deemed desirable (even possible) to have a consensus on all matters of intellectual or prudential judgment. Third, it is believed that growth and maturity can come about by fiat. As a consequence of the popularity of these misconceptions, we have recently seen a number of unfortunate events which violated lay competence in wholly "safe" areas. For instance, a "Catholic" lecture series is cancelled after external pressure upon the Ordinary because it is "too controversial," and the lay speakers are defamed by implication. A "Catholic" organization of outstanding experts is criticized when it advocates concrete application of ideas entirely consistent with Papal teaching, but which run counter to certain popular myths; the organization is "tamed" and subjected to tighter ecclesiastical control. Resolutions passed at meetings of certain large "Catholic" organizations are written beforehand, at headquarters. Lay professors are "cheap help" who are not given administrative responsibilities in certain educational establishments. *Etc.*

The point here is not that these examples describe a universal situation, for happily they do not. But they do indicate a pattern of lack of confidence and respect, and of denial of proper independence and responsibility. This pattern exists, in spite of crucially important exceptions, and the pattern has two dreadful consequences. First of all, the movement toward maturity is limited, for one cannot encourage the development of maturity in persons or organizations in this way. They require real freedom as a matter of their nature, enough freedom even to make some real mistakes. And secondly, this pattern ensures that the contact between the Catholics involved and the clergy is perfunctory, for the members of this group don't stand still when this is suggested in areas of their own competence. They know they don't have to; indeed, they must go on. When this rupture occurs, both sides lose enormously: the clergy because it loses intimate contact with one of the most vital forces in the Church; group X, as it might be called, because it becomes too far removed from the sacral, becomes truly "secularized."

Let us look at the quality of some contributions to the life of the Church made by the clergy. Again, we are not dealing with matters of faith and doctrine, but with the care and the depth used by the clergy in discharging its duties toward the laity, particularly toward the members of the group I have labelled "X." The central error here is the notion that the members of group X need no more from the clergy than the rest of the community does. But the opposite is true; members of group X need more help than the rest, and they need better help. Yet because of this mistaken notion, no adequate provision is made for the spiritual life of these people, and in fact the "usual" approaches are sometimes positively harmful for them.

For example, the life of the average parish is not at all at a level which can give members of group X what they need. Sermons are usually built around the catechism. This is simply not good enough. What these people need, and need badly, is to be preached the Gospel of Jesus Christ in all its glory and mystery. The common, the "liturgical" life is usually limited to the prayers after Mass. This, too, is not good enough. Parish activities, where the featured speaker is a football coach, are not good enough, nor are bazaars, nor novenas. In short, the typical parish life does not help them at all. At best it has no real impact; at worst it provides numerous occasions of sin, together with a great and deep sense of being outcast, and of being abandoned by the Church.

Similarly, the life of the diocese usually ignores the members of group X and makes no real provision for them (again there are important exceptions). For example, who is usually consulted on diocesan problems, or recognized in special ways? Rarely members

62

of group X. Why is the "family of the year" invariably characterized simply by an enormous number of children? Why not, for a
change, pick one whose father or mother wrote an important book?
Why is it that the annual appeal for funds for the Catholic University of America usually mentions only the training of priests
and nuns, and seldom, if ever, its outstanding departments where
scholars are trained, research is done, and books are written?

There is something deeply wrong here; a whole dimension seems
to be missing in the view the clergy have of their duty. I do not
advocate that every pastor be a scholar; quite the contrary. But one
must insist that he preach the Gospel, that he be a *pastor,* that he
give life. This the members of the "intellectual" group have a right
to. Let the hierarchy recognize explicitly and effectively that the
members of group X make a unique and essential contribution to
the Church and Society, and let them act accordingly. This is only
a matter of fairness.

The final and most important point concerns the potentialities
and difficulties of creative interaction. It is trite to say that laity
and clergy must try to understand each other better, but it is true
all the same. The members of group X must realize that the clergy
(and the hierarchy) are extraordinarily busy, just as busy as they
themselves are. Let them face the fact that the members of the
hierarchy adminster large and complicated organizations and do
this extremely well. Let them remember Gresham's law of public
administration: that the urgent problems crowd out the important
ones. Let them admit that when some action of the clergy fails to
hit the mark, when something "goes wrong," that it is more often
this phenomenon, perhaps together with inadequate "staff work,"
which produced the slip, rather than ill will, or deliberate intent.
In a word, let them not make impossible demands.

On the other side of the coin, let the members of the clergy realize that their administrative duties prevent them from being as thoughtful as they themselves would like to be. Let the clergy realize that they do have a pastoral duty to nourish the spirits of these strange "troublemakers," from among whom will come the great books, the discoveries, the music, of the future. Let the clergy realize that when members of group X criticize, this action is not personal, not vindictive, not self-seeking, not destructive. Rather let them see that these people have learned, through a discipline, an ascetic, lasting for many years, that only by the most searching, direct, and pressing questions is the truth ever found, is growth ever attained. Finally, let the clergy wake up to the fact that, to make real contact with group X, the clergy need only strive for its own highest ideals of charity, of selflessness, of service.

It is of crucial importance that group X not be left with a feeling of abandonment, nor the clergy with one of resentment. The two must find ways to speak to each other frankly, directly, and publicly. It will not do any longer to curse this problem behind closed doors. The health of the Church in this country is at stake, and only a radical willingness on both sides to look at the problem, and to seek mutually satisfactory procedures for its resolution will help. There are many concrete ways to implement such willingness. These range from informal consultation to the formation of permanent lay advisory bodies set up at various levels of Church organization. They include the encouraging of initiative and independence, and the open discussion of problem areas. Also the encouragement and recognition of members of the clergy close to (or in) group X could be important. But all hinges on this:

Let both the members of group X and of the clergy realize what they are about, that they have complementary roles to play in the life of the Church. Let them both know that they can play these roles adequately only if they strive to be true to their own vocations, to be true to their own ways of life.

VII

LAYMEN AND THEIR BISHOPS

Justus George Lawler

The spirit of reform and renewal in the Church has been profoundly stimulated by the preparatory work for the coming Council. The atmosphere is considerably clearer now than it was a decade ago when so masterful a work as Congar's *Vraie et fausse réforme* was withdrawn from circulation. Since Catholicism is an incarnational faith which must at once embrace the contingent multiplicity of history while remaining faithful to its own inner spiritual unity, the difficulties in every reform or renewal are the same as those encountered in any human act. "How shall we know the dancer from the dance?" asked the poet; how shall we live the changeless principles in a world of change? How shall we move in this world in harmonic response to the choreography of the other world?

What, in the light of this new spirit of reform, does one expect from the Second Vatican Council? I would suggest that we anticipate a strong impulse to be given to the entire awakening which the Christian community has experienced in the last fifty years.

This is a new theological era, Father William Lynch and others have declared; this does not mean there is a "new theology" in the pejorative sense. All theology is new: the Sacrament makes present; *now* is the acceptable time. And in point of fact the "new theological age" is no longer new in terms of chronology. For we are moving into the second stage of the modern Church, in which the achievements of the post-Vatican — and more definitely, the achievements of the post-Modernist — period will be coordinated, sheared of their extravagances, and given a new propulsion, a new energy: a stage in which the goal shall remain, as Blondel wrote to von Huegel, "not to metamorphose the traditional data but to deepen them."

Even in their American setting, religious doctrine and practice are moving towards a moment of synthesis. The liturgical revival, which in the hands of some of its more extreme partisans has occasionally appeared excessively taken up with group or mass participation is now emphasizing the need for that communion which Newman defined as "alone with the Alone," and which has recently been stressed in the Maritains' little book on prayer and contemplation. Theology for the laity is becoming a genuinely theological discipline, truly illuminated by the revolutionary advances being made in Scripture studies, and is no longer identified with the catechism-cum-metaphysics program of *A Companion to the Summa,* or with the retrogressive homeward-looking angelism of the recent compendium, *Theology in the Catholic College.*

Under the influence of kerygmatic catechetics the whole field of religious education from the primary grades up is being renovated. The "lay apostolate" is acquiring a fluidity of approach radically different from the rigid framework of its early days when European cadres of action were imported injudiciously, when such rudimentary notions as "think-judge-act" were subjected to a kind of rabbinic exegesis, and when the place of the Sodality in "Catholic Action" was a topic of urgent debate among our American "militants." One awaits, then, from the Council a summation and a clarification of the efforts of the last half century.

What might be hoped for from this Council — and I speak under correction and, of course, only for myself — is primarily not radical changes in the Church's organizational structure nor the resolution of a number of controverted questions of theology; as at Trent the guiding principle should be: "It is sufficient that the Council condemn the heresies, without judging all the disputes of the Schools." Certainly we await few definitions of doctrine in the strict sense, and we would expect whatever definitions may eventuate to be concerned with questions of the greatest *present* urgency.

The intellectual heirs of Veuillot and W. G. Ward are still active and still pressing for pronouncements on a multitude of questions. To these twentieth-century successors of the ultramontanists, we would say with Newman: "When has definition of doctrine *de fide* been a luxury of devotion and not a stern painful necessity?"

There is one specific area where there is a strong expectation of doctrinal pronouncements which shall complement those of the First Vatican Council, and which shall manifest that personal interpenetration of the two orders of the contingent and the absolute which is at the core of any lasting reform. At Vatican I the first constitution, *Pastor Aeternus,* on the papal primacy had been the subject of much discussion; the second constitution, *De Ecclesia Christi,* could not be taken up because of the dissolution of the Council. There is every reason to believe that this tract will be re-examined at Vatican II in the light of developments during the past ninety years. And in that light one can expect that certain topics which were to have been debated in 1870, such as the role of the episcopate and the place of the laity, will be clarified.

In that deepening and freshening of our comprehension of traditional beliefs, which will be the goal of the coming Council, the insights of the present moment of history will be invaluable. The whole drift of modern thought is away from the mechanistic orientation of the last three hundred years, and this personalist tenor has been reinforced by contemporary theological developments. The Church is not now envisioned primarily as an organizational entity, nor is the bishop regarded as some kind of ecclesiastical manager.

Even that sacrament which lends itself most readily to being defined in juridic terms, Penance, has been shown by Adrienne von Speyr's *Die Beichte* to entail a personal encounter with the life of the Trinity. The insights of existentialism, of the meeting of the "self with the other," of the "I and thou," have been confirmed both in the doctrine of the Mystical Body and in the notion of Christ as the archetype of the sacraments.

I am in no way qualified to discuss how these various renewed insights will affect the theology of the episcopal state, but speaking as a layman, I do feel there will be consequences in the practical order of such a theological formulation which ought to be examined. First, one would expect the cardinalate to be reduced to a purely curial or honorary status (as presently with papal chamberlains), and the election of the Chief Bishop to be confined exclusively to certain bishops representing the episcopate of the whole Church.

That an accident of medieval polity affecting the ancient see of Rome could in the twentieth century result in the election of the supreme teacher by members of the Church-taught is to depreciate both symbolically and in fact the episcopal college. How such a reform would be implemented is a minor consideration: possibly primatial sees, or — where none exists as in this country — major dioceses would have attached to them the right of voting in the conclave.

Second, the legal fiction of "titular" bishops could be discontinued. Auxiliary bishops now function mainly as subordinate governing officials or as ministers of Confirmation; but since the episcopal state is not primarily an administrative office, and since Confirmation need not be conferred by a bishop, this notion of a "titular" bishop reduces the episcopal consecration to a kind of honorific. One remedy would be to allow lesser prelates to act as the bishop's auxiliaries, or — the preferable solution — to break up the largest dioceses so that titular bishops, unless coadjutors, could govern their own sees; the present meaningless situation in which a bishop may be pastor of a local parish could thus be terminated.

Finally, the essence of the episcopal office will be clarified. According to one of the best commentaries on ecclesiastical law (Abbo and Hannan) the common opinion of canonists is that the bishop should be more skilled in canon law than learned in theology. This judgment may indicate special pleading on the part of canonists, but one suspects rather that its general acceptance is an effect of that denigration of the episcopate which Cardinal Manning in his later years decried as "Catholic presbyterianism." The bishop becomes in that misconception not a teacher in his own right, but merely the emissary of the Pope. And through this distortion of traditional teaching, he becomes in this country the victim of those arrogant attacks on the "Roman hierarchy" as the "Vatican foreign services," which still emanate from Protestants and Others and from the half-lights of the Beacon Press.

But these attacks may be as much the result of the failure of theologians to explicate Catholic teaching as of prejudice on the part of non-Catholics. For Catholic teaching affirms that the bishop is not the Pope's vicar, much less his ambassador: he is the one teacher of his *ecclesia,* and as a member of the episcopal college he is a teacher of the universal Church in union with its Chief Bishop.

One might further suggest that it has been this notion of the bishop as an interpreter of the law rather than as a teacher of doctrine which accounts for the not infrequent silence of some bishops on pressing social and ethical issues, such as desegregation and disarmament. If the bishop is the chief teacher of Christian truth, he is also its chief witness; but if he is regarded as an interpreter of the law, his proper domain is jurisprudence, not testimony to truth.

It is not desirable to discount any claims of prudence; but to make them the overriding consideration, and to define the episcopal office in terms of them, may tend to induce a muteness that occasionally verges on the scandalous. The "church of silence" is not always behind the iron curtain.

Furthermore a witness is a martyr. This martyrdom may not be a murder in the cathedral; it may take the more harrowing form of public criticism, as it did recently in New Orleans; it may take the form of the antagonism of some of the bishop's brethren; it may take the form — as it did in more than a few instances at the time of Vatican I — of rebuke by the Pope; or it may take the form of loss of one's see, as in a notable case in this hemisphere. But may not this be the price of accepting the plentitude of the priesthood, and of being the successor of the apostles?

However, it must be said in all fairness that the American Church has been blessed with bishops who for the most part were sympathetic to the legitimate aspirations of the community, and who, particularly from the time of Gibbons and Ireland, have identified themselves with the cause of social justice. Unfortunately in recent decades these were often causes initiated outside the Church, and the hierarchy merely gave its approbation to movements already sanctioned by public opinion. This tended to confirm in the non-Catholic mind the crude maxim that "the Vatican always follows the election returns." But at least our bishops have never been mere ceremonial functionaries: they could not be described, to use Monsignor Duchesne's mordant phrase, as "mitred sacristans."

There have been eminent theologians and humanists among them, such as the two Kenricks and Spalding of Peoria. And coming from the ranks of the middle-class, they have very rarely been intent on that social display enshrined in Archbishop Seton's monument to ecclesiastical snobbism, *Memories of Many Years;* nor have they been afflicted with that passion for personal aggrandizement which led Léon Bloy to observe of an eminent prelate: "The Cardinal had a heart of gold. Solid gold."

But one regrets having to state that the bishops have not always exercised that leadership which their personal qualities, their educational training, and their consecration authorized. This failure has stemmed both from the lack of "self-knowledge" which the truncated theology of 1870 induced, and from the same difficulties of articulation and communication that beset the heads of all large institutions and corporations: they are faced with the problem of keeping in vital contact with all the echelons of their organization.

It is here that the layman plays an indispensable role. Some formalized instrument ought to be established so that the bishop, who necessarily moves in a circle of high public officials and of people of wealth and power, may hear the word of the layman, and may encounter through him the issues before the mass of the

Christian community. I say "formalized instrument" because the present make-shift arrangement of Communion Breakfasts or Holy Name affairs or semi-solemn receptions, or even the presence of the layman on the staffs of some diocesan papers, is much too indirect and haphazard to result in any real communication.

There is a parallel to the kind of formal institution of the dialogue, which I am suggesting, in the quinquennial assemblies at which the bishops gathered with the lower clergy in the church of France before the revolution — the gap between bishop and clergy at that period being greater than the gap between hierarchy and laity in the present age. One would like, for instance, to see the layman represented at the meetings of the N.C.W.C. or at diocesan synods: and this, not merely as the spokesman of the present narrow conception of the "lay apostolate," but as the voice of all the interests and hopes of the Church, as seen from the vantage of the lay state.

Such a move might entail stripping away some of the vestigial protocol and panoply that new encumber the bishop in the exercise of his office. And it means that the layman's testimony is not always going to be couched in diplomatic niceties. The layman must speak vigorously and clearly; indeed, this vigor and clarity are the outward signs of his inward commitment to the cause of the Church in the temporal order, and they ought not to be interpreted as indications of a lack of obedience or docility.

From the viewpoint of doctrine the bishop's role is primarily "preceptive," that is, the bishop is first of all a teacher. But his role is also "receptive," that is, the bishop must "consult" the faithful. Newman certainly over-emphasized this "consultation," but nevertheless he was nearer to the authentic tradition than such contemporary theologians as Franzelin who regarded the faithful as simply the passive mirrors of official teaching. The layman must take an active part in the elucidation of doctrine and morality, and he is obliged to proffer his testimony even if it is ignored or if the only apparent response it elicits is a reprimand for effrontery and lack of "respect."

The bishop is a pontiff: a builder of bridges. One of the bridges that the forthcoming Council of the bishops should repair is that between hierarchy and laity. This can be accomplished only after there has been elaborated a genuine theology of the episcopal office and of the lay state.

VIII

FAILURES — LAY AND CLERICAL

William J. Nagle

My contention is that Catholic laymen have failed miserably in their work of bringing Christ — God Incarnate — into the world. And I submit that a large part of the reason for that failure is that they have not understood their role in the Church.

The liturgy remains the best example of this failure. All of the recent liturgical reforms are aimed at getting the layman back to his rightful role in the Mass — fully participating, fully understanding, fully worshipping. This cannot, of course, be done overnight. The basic action of the Mass, the interaction of love, has been encrusted over, obscured, for centuries. Now the crust is being removed, and lay people are again emerging as that *plebs sancta*, that consecrated people of which the Canon of the Mass speaks. We still have a long way to go, of course, but the significant fact is that in principle at least the place of the layman in worship has been recognized.

In practice, however, we in the United States have been slow in embracing these reforms. Why? In part the lag may be due to a somewhat narrow, overly conservative outlook on the part of many of our bishops and priests, who have not themselves kept up with the liturgical studies that have formed the bases for these recent reforms. But if blame must be placed, we would have to admit that laymen have also not done their part. They have not greeted these reforms with any great enthusiasm, and they have not urged their pastors to follow Rome's lead.

Laymen as well as clerics must be prepared to do a substantial amount of studying if they are to appreciate fully what is happening in the Church today, in this matter of the Church's worship and many other things. Only if the layman becomes knowledgeable about his role will he be able to articulate his desires, for the vernacular or anything else, to his pastor, to his bishop, to church officials in Rome. And there is certainly no point in encouraging laymen to be more articulate if they are not knowledgeable.

The need for knowledge is not the only problem. According to Yves Congar, there is a sense in which the layman up to fairly recent times can be said to have been a proletarian in the Church — at least in the way that Arnold Toynbee uses the word. A proletarian, says Toynbee, is not made by being in a subordinate condition, but by living in a society of which he does not himself feel to be organically an active member with his own rights. Laymen seem now to be on their way to becoming organically active members again, by right and by fact. But in the ecclesiastical, institutional structure — in what for want of a better term we might refer to as Church government — the layman has a long distance to travel if he is to obtain even some of the rights he had in the Church in earlier centuries.

The fact is, I think, that our present means for developing and channeling public opinion in the Church are quite inadequate. Indeed, at this stage there is a positive lack of public opinion in the Church; lay people simply do not articulate their thoughts and desires, and a serious lack of communication exists between the laity and the hierarchy in this country.

The point can perhaps be best illustrated by example. There has been so little discussion within the Church between laymen, priests and bishops about the whole basis of the Catholic school system that when a serious public policy issue arose over aid to Catholic schools the bishops did not in fact speak for a substantial number of laymen. At the time of the vote on President Kennedy's school bill, eight of the eleven Catholic Democrats in the Senate were on record as approving the bill. These eight senators (and significantly large numbers of other Catholic laymen) were apparently not in agreement with the recommendation of the Chairman of the NCWC Administrative Board that we oppose any education bill that did not include aid to Catholic schools.

I cite this matter here only to point up the fact that on this most important issue — which touches in some way the lives of practically all of the Catholics in the U.S. — there has not been sufficient discussion within the Church. When the issue arose publicly, the bishops who spoke could hardly do so out of a consensus of the Catholic citizenry; no consensus had been formed because the discussion, debate and thought required for forming a consensus had not taken place.

During the school aid debate many Catholic spokesmen stressed the fact that the primary responsibility for their children's education belongs to the parent, not to the state. The point is an important one, but the state is not the only agency in need of this reminder. If it is the parents who have the primary responsibility, the faculties in our Catholic schools teach by their delegation. It would seem, then, that the thoughts and opinions of the parents about the way their parish schools are run, about the policies of a diocesan education office, or the national education policies of NCWC are very much in order.

I cite the need for public opinion within the Church on this matter of education, not simply because of its topicality as a public issue but because I think it is over the whole issue of education that Catholic lay people in the United States are most likely to begin to express their opinions. It is also one of the issues over which they seem most frustrated.

The lack of communication between lay people and the hierarchy is similarly evident in another crucial area. To state my point as frankly and honestly as I can: I see very little evidence that our bishops and priests realize that for the vast majority of Catholic married couples the most serious moral problems revolve around the questions of rhythm and birth control.

These couples are not asking the bishops for permission to use artificial contraceptives; they would ask (if they would only speak out) that the hierarchy and Catholic universities and medical schools do all that is scientifically possible to make rhythm more workable. On the theoretical level, married couples would ask theologians to devote more attention to the theology of marriage; they would ask bishops, theologians and philosophers to take a more careful look at our natural law argument against contraceptives.

Monsignor Irving DeBlanc, formerly director of NCWC's Family Life Bureau, has cited a study by a North Carolina statistician which indicated that Catholic married couples use contraceptive methods of birth control about as often as non-Catholics. Whatever the accuracy of his figures, can we say that the remaining percentage — whether it be fifty per cent, thirty per cent, or seventy per cent — are not using contraceptives because they are convinced such use is against the natural law?

I have taken no scientific polls, but my guess would be that the majority of American Catholic married couples who are not practicing birth control are simply following the direction of the Church rather than any strong conviction about the validity of the natural law argument. These Catholic couples are practicing rhythm — and are having more children — because, as commonly articulated, the Church says rhythm is morally acceptable under certain conditions and contraceptives are not morally acceptable under any conditions.

Let me make myself quite clear. I am not questioning the basic validity of the natural law argument on birth control. I am suggesting that the mere repetition of formulas stated centuries ago is not very convincing, and I find somewhat puzzling the head-in-the-sand posture of Catholic moralists on this question. Even in its most imperfect present form, rhythm could be presented in a positive way — as a means to sanctity, instead of with the usual negative approach of implying that if a couple is not perfect enough to rely completely on the providence of God, they are *permitted* to use rhythm.

I said I saw very little evidence that our bishops and priests realize that the most serious moral problems for the vast majority of Catholic married couples revolve around the questions of rhythm and birth control. That may seem a strong statement, but how else can we explain the fact that in recent years leading Catholic universities have turned down foundation grants for study on rhythm and population control on the ground that the subject is "too controversial"? How else can we explain the fact that our priests and bishops, by and large, have similarly ignored the problem, although sociologists warn us that birth control is one of the major sources of leakage from the Church?

Marriage, I fear, was largely given over to the canonists some centuries ago; only in our own age are theologians beginning to realize that marriage is the means through which most men gain their salvation, and even now progress in this area often seems slow and halting. What I am trying to stress is that laymen have not received the kind of theological and moral guidance on these most important questions that they need to sanctify themselves, their families and the world, and — more to the point here — they have not been insistent enough in asking for that guidance.

Some months ago, Bishop Jan van Dodewaard of Haarlem, The Netherlands, urged laymen "to stimulate or even to press Catholic theologians to give their full attention to questions which urgently call for solution." And this is the point: we cannot simply sit back as disgruntled proletarians. We must communicate with our bishops, with our theologians. And if the channels of communication sometimes seem to be disconnected on the other end, we have to keep on until we are sure churchmen are listening and understanding. This is not simply our right — it is our duty.

I am convinced that unless we Catholic laymen understand and begin to fulfill our role in the Church we shall not be prepared to fulfill our role in temporal society either.

As Canon Leclercq writes: "What the Christian social movement has lacked has been laymen 'taking the temporal order seriously,' that is, applying their minds to the social problem in its own right. There have been a few such men, but they lacked the religious formation which would have enabled them to approach secular questions from an inherently Christian point of view. . . . The good Christian has always had the impression that he was not a fully satisfactory follower of Christ if he took the temporal order with absolute seriousness and that he who did so was only a lukewarm Christian. It seemed that no one could be both wholly Christian and wholly lay."

The fact is that the Christian function of the layman is determined by his situation in the world, that is, by his natural commitment to the work of the world, which we do not give up in order to serve God's kingdom. We give glory to God not by withholding ourselves from that work but precisely in it and through it. Christ lives in the world, is present in the world, in and through us.

Yves Congar makes the necessary point forcefully when he says: "At bottom, forgetfulness of the true role of lay people leads both to clericalism in the Church, and to laicism in the world. Pastorally, clericalism results in this, that lay people, kept in subjection and passivity in the Church, are not formed for their own Christian responsibilities, which it is their business to discharge in the world and in the course of history." Only that layman can fill his role who is informed, who is fully aware of the requirements of the Christian conscience, who reacts spontaneously not as a sectarian Catholic but as a fully formed person filled with Christ.

For the most part the lead in those areas concerned with justice and charity in the social and political order has been taken by secularists; for the most part Catholic laymen (though in the U.S. we number forty million-plus) have not taken the lead. Pope Pius XII urged laymen to show courage, the courage of initiative. As Congar says, lay people have the right and the duty to become "adult Christians, free men," and the adult "is a man who no longer has to be warned, encouraged, supervised in order that he may act." When are we going to stop looking over our shoulders for direction from our priests? When are we going to act like adults?

I would end with two points. The first is that in this whole area of the layman in the Church and the world, we must realize that we are in an early stage of development. Most of the books specifically addressed to the subject have been published only in the last six years, and there is yet to be an American book on the subject. At this stage it seems to me that the role of the individual layman is much clearer than that of Catholic organizations.

Following the direction of Popes Pius XI and Pius XII on the subject of Catholic Action, we now generally speak of Catholic Action as the "collaboration of the laity in the apostolate of the hierarchy" — that is, some group acting under a specific mandate from the bishop to promote some specific religious end of the bishop's apostolate. We speak of the "organized lay apostolate" as engaging in activities deriving from "the mission of the Church," and this lay apostolate is by definition lay directed. However, the difficulty is that many of our lay organizations — some of them founded years ago before any such distinctions were understood or even made — have a schizoid character; they seem, because of some tie to the bishop or chancery office, to be Catholic Action groups, while some of their activities and ends are more definitely in the lay apostolate area.

On this and similar questions, and indeed on the whole question of the layman in the Church, the Second Vatican Council might lead to further definition. Meanwhile, we must recognize that some of the strains connected with the striving of the layman for his rightful status in the Church are appearing first in certain lay organizations, and that this strain is probably inevitable in a transitional stage such as this one.

My second and final point is directed not to the question of lay organizations and the confusion surrounding them at the present time, but to laymen as individuals. It must be realized that there is something of an "occupational hazard" incurred when one reads in this field and involves himself deeply in these very fundamental questions about his place in the Church and his role as a Catholic layman in society. Here I would express a personal warning: dipping only slightly into the literature in this area may lead to a considerable degree of frustration as one comes to realize that there does exist a gap — and for the time, I fear, a growing gap — between the educated laity and the clergy.

I sense in the United States at this point the growth of a new anticlericalism. It does not have the secular roots of the anticlericalism of the Continent. Its source is rather in the frustration, the disenchantment, the disillusionment of many lay Catholics who have somewhere caught a glimpse of what the Church should be and of what they should be in the Church, and who are now painfully aware of the gap between the ideal and the reality.

As a result of this situation, what might be termed the "deinstitutionalized Catholic" has become quite common among educated laymen. Such a Catholic is one who goes to Mass and the Sacraments but who has retreated from "involvement" in the institutional Church or even in Catholic organizations. To my mind, the increase of "deinstitutionalized Catholics" among the very laymen who should be leaders presents one of the most serious problems facing the Church in the United States. And I consider the problem especially serious because I see very little evidence that our ecclesiastical leaders are even aware it exists.

IX

PROBLEMS AND POSSIBILITIES

Daniel Callahan

It is impossible to talk about the status of the laity in the Church today without talking about the relationship of laity and clergy. Yet however one chooses to characterize that relationship, one is bound to be struck by a number of curiosities. The most patent in recent years was the establishment by Pope John XXIII of a preparatory commission on the lay apostolate for the forthcoming Council. For the first time in the history of the Church, the question of the laity had been given a status equal to that of the traditional matters which have concerned ecumenical councils. But it very soon became clear that no provisions were to be made for lay consultants or advisers to that commission.

The commission thus had the curious distinction that it was the only one in which none of those who will be affected directly by its work were represented. A theological commission without theologians or a commission on the missions without missionaries would have been unthinkable. In contrast, hardly a word was spoken about the omission of laymen from the deliberations of the preparatory commission on the laity; it was accepted as a matter of course. One need hardly add that no laymen will be participants in the Council itself.

No one, of course, is surprised by these omissions. For many cen-

84

turies the layman has had no direct role to play in the highest deliberations of the Church. Neither Canon Law nor recent tradition encourages such a role. If the very fact that a commission on the laity was formed is revolutionary, the exclusion of the laity from it is merely the faithful following of modern tradition. The importance of the laity was dramatically recognized; the importance of the contribution they might make in a preparatory commission was not.

This combination of revolution in one direction and close adherence to custom in another perfectly symbolizes the problem of the laity in the Church today. For the problem is one which goes well beyond the usual diagnoses and appraisals. It is not only, as is often said, a matter of the clergy becoming less paternalistic, less authoritarian, and more open to the needs and talents of the laity. Nor is it only a matter of stimulating the laity to be more active and energetic in serving the Church. To be sure, all these things are needed. But what is needed even more is a sharp awareness that, as the Church is structured today, none of those advances would guarantee a viable and integral place for the laity. None, moreover, would guarantee that the awakening aspirations of the laity would fully be met.

To put it directly, the Church is in the midst of a revolution with which it does not have the means, juridical or theological, to cope. The revolution has been long in the making — both clergy and laity have contributed to bringing it about. From the clerical side, the innumerable exhortations of recent popes that the laity become more active in the service of the Church, the work of important clerics on the theology of the laity, and the widespread desire of many bishops, pastors and priests for lay assistance have been a major influence. From the lay side, the emergence of an educated class of laymen, the heeding of papal and episcopal words, and a general rebirth of Christian spirituality have all made a profound difference. Taken together, these developments are nothing less than revolutionary.

But what has been the result of this ferment? Very little, it would appear. For the most part the revolution remains one of attitude, expectation and aspiration — not one of profound change in the Church itself. The Church, it becomes increasingly obvious, is not geared for this comparatively sudden development. For decades the Church's organizational and institutional life has been the sole responsibility of the clergy: from the teaching office of the Church down to the most remote parish everything of importance has been in the hands of the clergy. The absence of laymen from the preparatory commission on the laity simply typifies, in a singular fashion, the present relationship of laity and clergy. Even in those matters which directly concern the laity, the laity are, for the most part, not consulted.

The one conclusion that ought not to be drawn from these facts is that the hierarchy and clergy are engaged in a great conspiracy to keep the layman in his place. This is hardly reasonable, hardly fair. It is much more to the point to recognize how centuries of custom have brought about the present situation; to recognize, that is, that the present generation of clergy (and laity) have been nurtured and shaped by a long tradition of seeing the laity as inactive, decidedly silent members of the Church. Even more to the point, there is little in Canon Law which would appear to sanction the laity's playing a fuller role in the Church. Canonically, there is little to encourage the clergy to give the laity more freedom and responsibility; there is simply no provision at all for the layman to exercise some special role of his own.

Indeed, I think it particularly necessary to recognize that Canon Law spells out in great detail the duties and obligations of the clergy; it scarcely mentions the rights of the laity. The effect of this one-sided stress is to offer little in the way of encouragement to the priest or bishop who might feel inclined to grant greater independence to the laymen under his jurisdiction; the major responsibilities are his and he is the one accountable.

Caution, under these circumstances, is only natural. Nothing enjoins the clergy to delegate responsibility; on the contrary, almost everything enjoins him not to, if only as the course of care and prudence. The inevitable outcome of this canonical situation has been merely to reinforce historical and sociological trends: the isolation of seminary training, the social and educational gap between laity and clergy, and the development of a paternalistic attitude on the part of the clergy and one of passivity on the part of the laity.

This is not to say that the clergy could not do more than they already do; clearly they could. But it does suggest that the supposed tension existing between laity and clergy can easily be misunderstood — if only because there are so many priests who do want the laity to take a more active role. Yet their hands are often as effectively tied — by Canon Law, their bishops, or by their pastors (in the instance of zealous young curates) — as those of the laity. Moreover, many of the supposed lay-clerical tensions often turn out to be tensions of an entirely different order: conflict between liberals and conservatives, younger generation and older, liturgists and mariologists, pluralistic and ghetto Catholics. Nevertheless, despite these important qualifications, it is inescapable that there is an imbalance between laity and clergy in the Church.

The net impact of this imbalance, while innocuous enough in

earlier centuries, has been, in our time, to bring about an increasingly delicate situation. Given the present status of the laity in the Church, it is exceedingly difficult to see how, in fact, lay aspirations can be realized. It is no less difficult to see how clerical aspirations for a more effective, integrated laity can be realized either. Without some fundamental canonical changes and theological development the most that can be hoped for would be slow, halting and probably meager improvements. As things stand now, lay aspiration is for the most part in direct conflict with possibility.

What aggravates this conflict, making it significantly different from similar ones in other eras, is that both education and clerical exhortation have led the layman to set very high goals. It is hardly too much to say that many of the clergy have goaded the laity into expecting and asking for very much from the Church. The laity have done their own part in raising their sights but, on the whole, it is the theologians — indeed, popes and bishops — who have taken the lead in pressing for a fuller participation of the laity in the Church.

The dangerous part of the conflict between aspiration and possibility lies in the fact that laymen are increasingly being led to expect to play a role which the Church is in no position to let them play. The layman has been incited by the Church to ask for, and anticipate, a freedom and responsibility which, in the end, the contemporary Church is hardly prone to give him. Just as aspiration conflicts with possibility, so too expectation conflicts with probability. Nothing good can come from conflicts of this sort; on the contrary, considerable harm seems an inevitable result.

One obvious result could be anticlericalism. If the clergy leads the laity to expect changes which it is, in the end, prevented from bringing about (or unwilling in practice to bring about) much good will between laity and clergy is bound to be lost. The clergy will then have done little more than help to create a profoundly frustrated, disenchanted laity. The whole trend in recent decades has been (in theory mainly) toward greater responsibility for the laity: if this responsibility is not in fact given, the results will be far worse than if there had been no movement in the first place.

A reaction has already, to some extent, begun to set in. It can be seen, if the signs will be read, in the unwillingness of many recent Catholic college graduates to join parish or Church organizations; in the flight from Catholic higher education of many young Catholic scholars; in the transference of the zeal of many apostolic Catholics from Church to secular organizations; in the desire of innumerable Catholics to detach themselves from any cultural attachment to the Church, to lose themselves in a sheltering, pluralistic society.

The one distinctive thing that is likely to characterize this anticlericalism — though a-clericalism might be a more precise term — is that it will be the product of thwarted dreams, frustrated hopes, and confounded apostolic zeal. But anticlericalism is only the worst side of the picture; at the very least, the whole lay apostolate could simply wither away to a feeble, insignificant movement, of little consequence to the ongoing life of the Church. The only possibility for a genuinely effective lay apostolate is a clergy willing and *able* to give laymen both the freedom and respect — and independence — in non-dogmatic matters, needed to make the apostolate viable and attractive.

There is still another dimension to the lay-clerical relationship. One of the great and persistent problems of the Church is to keep popular piety consistent with theological developments. The traditional lag between the work of the theologians and the religious opinions of the people, while somewhat supportable in the past, cannot be afforded today. The liturgical movement, the social teachings of the Church, catechetics, and the Biblical revival have all suffered from this lag. Important and necessary advances have frequently suffered the fate of lay indifference or even hostility. A laity closely attuned to new developments, a laity working harmoniously with the clergy could help provide the kind of popular response to change lacking in the past.

The picture I have painted so far may seem unrelievedly dark, the possibilities of genuine progress slight. Given only the present structure of the Church, and given only the imbalance between lay aspirations and ecclesiastical reality, there would be little to justify much optimism. Fortunately, there is much more to be said. There is, despite its limitations, the unprecedented establishment of the preparatory commission of the lay apostolate; there is the work of many theologians on the theological problem of the laity; there is the increasing (if not dramatic) reliance of many bishops and priests on lay assistance. There is, most importantly, the undoubted loyalty of the laity to the Church.

The one thing that saves the American Church from classical anticlericalism is that lay desires are not based on ideals counter to those of the Church; they stem from ideals thoroughly Catholic in origin and content. They stem from ideals held by the Church and affirmed by the Church — but which are not put into practice. The great danger is not loss of faith. The great danger is that of a loss of hope and interest, a loss of zeal and idealism. This would be a grievous loss to the Church, a grievous spiritual loss to those laymen who have staked so much on the future of the lay movement.

Here lies the importance of the Second Vatican Council. It is within the power of the Council to bring about effective reforms, to make those changes which will give both clergy and laity wider scope of action and greater self-responsibility. It can, if it will, do even more: it could, conceivably, give the layman some consultative role in the magisterium itself. There are both historical precedents and common sense reasons to support some move in this direction. The only real hope for an effective, engaged, active laity is that, by some means, they be given a hearing on those hierarchical decisions which intimately concern them, a hearing on those matters which bear directly on their needs, capacities and talents. The great challenge of the Council is to find means to bring this goal about without sacrificing that necessary authority which must always remain in the hands of the hierarchy and clergy.

There is no reason why a trained, loyal, integrated laity should in any respect pose a threat to the authority of the Church or its divinely ordained means of teaching and preserving the deposit of faith. There is, even more, no sound reason to assume that the laity would abuse any greater freedom given them. It ought to be within the genius of the Church to find ways of preserving the authority and office of the clergy while at the same time increasing the freedom and self-responsibility of the laity.

The desire of the laity today is only that the clergy engage in some careful soul-searching; that the Council give its utmost attention not only to a more effective utilization of the laity in the Church's mission to the world but also to the needs of the laity with respect to the inner life of the Church. To even face the problems and needs suggested here, much less to find solutions to them, will require much boldness. But it is a boldness not impossible for the Church.

CONTRIBUTORS

James O'Gara, co-founder of *Today* magazine, is managing editor of *The Commonweal.*

Monsignor John Tracy Ellis, author of *American Catholics and the Intellectual Life* and other works, is Professor of Church History at the Catholic University of America.

Father Robert W. Hovda is a member of the Department of Religion at the Catholic University of America.

Philip Scharper is chief editor for the publishing house of Sheed & Ward.

Joseph E. Cunneen, managing editor of *Cross Currents,* is a member of the faculty of St. Peter's College, New Jersey.

John B. Mannion is the executive secretary of the Liturgical Conference.

Charles M. Herzfeld, a regular contributor to Catholic journals, is in charge of ballistic missile defense research at the Pentagon.

Justus George Lawler, author of *The Catholic Dimension in Higher Education,* is a member of the faculty at St. Xavier College, Chicago, and editor for Herder and Herder.

William J. Nagle, the editor of *Morality and Modern Warfare,* is a research analyst in Washington.

Daniel Callahan, co-editor of *Christianity Divided,* is an associate editor of *The Commonweal.*

Praise for
Swim the Lake Before You Row the Boat

"I love, love, love this book! I am committed to following the Formula with my grandson. And I am buying copies for my 2 sets of parents of my grandkids (yes, including the ones with granddaughters only) and for friends with sons/grandsons! I couldn't help but think, as we watched the news about yet another school shooting, that if the Flying Eagle Formula were instituted in the schools it would make a world of real difference and save lives far beyond the other measures they want to take."

—CANDY McCUNE, grandparent, attorney and entrepreneur,
www.guidemetobetterhealth.com

"I love this book! I was burned out and ready to leave teaching! I was tired of doing things that just weren't working for kids. No kidding. I had already applied for a job at a gas company. And then I read this book and am so excited again about teaching! THIS is the answer! Every teacher needs to read this book!"

—KIM COFFMAN, teacher, special education

"This book has come out at the right time, in the right place! My biggest fear is my son growing up in a world that condemns success, and him buying into the brainwashing. *Swim the Lake Before You Row the Boat* is a masterclass for entrepreneurs who want to ensure their sons get the right message and learn the road to confidence. It is a race for our sons' minds, and if you want to win that race you need this book as your race car!"

—RAY BREHM, entrepreneur and best-selling author

"An inspiring "blueprint" for what I'd like to bring into our lives to enrich my kids' growth and childhood. It's like you figured out what the experts have been studying and trying to tell us for decades."

—KENDRA, Mom of two

"*Swim the Lake Before You Row the Boat* provides life lessons on how to instill a strong foundation in boys that will enable them to build a successful life–regardless of the path they choose. These are turbulent times. This book is your guide to shape a boy's life, guide his soul and set his successful destiny."
— TOM WATKINS, former Michigan State Mental Health Director and State Superintendent of Public Education

"*Swim the Lake* is a beautiful book, to help you create a pathway for yourself and the boys in your life. This is a book which all teachers, parents and those that want to make their communities stronger should read as they journey. It's accessible and something I know I will come back to over and over. It captures the wisdom of the age old and translates beautifully to our ever changing world. It is a literary life compass. It has stories which will move you, models which structure your actions and a message that will stay with you, helping yourself and others live a successful, sustainable life that inspires."
— DAVE STRUDWICK, Educational Innovator, Founder of Schools and CoCreator of the Blackawton Bees, the world's youngest published scientists

SWIM

— *the lake* —

BEFORE YOU ROW

— *the boat* —

Awaken a Boy's Success Mindset,
Unleash His Confidence and
Give Him the Foundation for a Great Life

TESS & DEBORAH CANJA

SPENCER WHITE
PUBLISHING

SPENCER WHITE
PUBLISHING

Swim the Lake Before You Row the Boat
ISBN 978-1-7338372-0-0 (paperback)
ISBN 978-1-7338372-1-7 (ebook)

For information: Spencer White Publishing, 2025 Central Park Drive, Ste 285, Okemos, MI 48805.

Edited by Barbara Munson, Munson Communications Editorial Services
Interior design by Monica Thomas for TLC Book Design, *TLCBookDesign.com*

Camp photos by Alex, Tess and Deb Canja. Photos of Tess & Alex on page 24 by "Pop" Palmer. Stock photos by *Adobestock.com*: cover, lake water ©klikk; page 166, toolbox ©donatas1205.

Library of Congress Control Number: 2019943594

Printed in the United States of America

*This book is dedicated to Brian and Scott,
the light of our lives,
and to all those who want the children in their lives
to become happy, productive and successful
members of a better world…*

*and to Alex,
who did his best to help make that happen…*

and to all the boys who swam the lake…

and all who will.

TABLE *of* CONTENTS

FOREWORD

I wish I'd had this book when my sons were growing up. Camp Flying Eagle was closed by then and even though my boys ran around the camp grounds and had many camp-like adventures, that's not the experience that gives the "success identity."

In fact, when I look back on my parenting, I can see that I was trying my best to give them a lifetime of advantage, but I just didn't know how. I wanted to be a good parent. I read parenting books. I was the den mother to a huge group of Tiger Cubs, and then Cub Scouts and then Webelos. I ran after-school programs for the entire elementary school so that my kids could benefit from having enriching experiences with their classmates by learning different languages and dissecting frogs and building bottle rockets. When they hit middle school, I was the Science Olympiad Coach and for four years they had a chance to be on a team and win competitions. I went to about a million soccer games. I sent them to summer camp, to NASA Space Camp and to Computer/Gaming Camp.

I was doing all of those things to give my boys a great start in life. What I know now is that as great as all of those things are, and they do help, they aren't the most important. Sometimes it's only when you look back and analyze things from a distance that suddenly things become so much clearer. I wish I had realized then what I know now. My greatest wish is that you will have the clarity that I didn't have in order to give your sons the real lifetime of advantage.

"But...isn't love enough?" I've heard people ask. I wish I could say yes. But I can't, and here's why. Look back at your own life. Most of us can say with certainty that our parents loved us. But a lot of us can then add, "in their own way." And others of us know that they did a lot of things we wish they hadn't. Things they may have thought were loving or in our best interest, but in the end, they weren't.

Our good intentions are not enough. We need to combine our good intentions with a vision of the result we want our parenting to produce and a specific, proven plan for getting there.

What type of a future do you want for your son? Do you want to HOPE that what you do will be good enough, loving enough, supportive enough to help your son navigate peer pressure, guns, drugs, sex, and the everyday stress that boys face today? Or do you want to do everything you can now to ensure they WILL grow up to become successful, happy, well-adjusted, and compassionate husbands, fathers and community members?

That's why we wrote this book.

May Your Journey Be Blessed,
Deb

PROLOGUE

I'm ninety-two years old now, but I was eighty-three when I started writing this book with nothing more than an idea and a dream. I guess that shows that it is never too late to follow your dreams.

When I look back on my life, I'm surprised that some of the things I did had a greater impact than I ever imagined they would. I have learned that any of us can make a profound and positive difference at any time.

In 1956, as a young married couple with two small children, my husband, Alex, and I took a leap of faith and bought a summer camp for boys on beautiful Crooked Lake in Northern Michigan. Although the American Camping Association called our camp "exemplary" and "exceptionally fine," the real gift came many years later when we heard from former campers and counselors who told us that we, and the Camp Flying Eagle experience, had changed their lives in positive ways that had a lasting impact.

This is the story of our secret to creating the magic in the lives of young boys that puts them on a path to becoming wonderful fathers, husbands, teachers, and community leaders. I want to share it because if we could do it, so can you. And our world surely needs more fine young men.

The magic of Camp Flying Eagle lives on in the hearts and minds of the boys and men who shared it with us and who have passed it along to their sons and families. I hope it will live on here, too, in lessons passed on to those you love.

All best wishes and love,
Tess

Tess and grandsons Brian and Scott at Crooked Lake

PART ONE

CREATE A PATTERN *of* SUCCESS

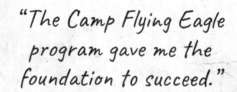

"The Camp Flying Eagle
program gave me the
foundation to succeed."

Bob, camper 1968–1976
Top rated government contract attorney, retired U.S. Coast Guard
Commander, happily married, two loving daughters,
board member of local non-profit organization

CHAPTER ONE

ATTRACT SUCCESS

Snow was falling outside our classroom and the night was cold and dark. It was the winter of 1993 and even though I had long since graduated from high school, college, and even law school, here I was sitting at a desk in a familiar-looking high school classroom with a bunch of other parents. Our eyes were glued to a video playing on a small TV perched on one of those rolling carts they have in schools. We were there to participate in a program about drug abuse prevention called "Parent-to-Parent."

Two volunteer parent trainers stood at the front of the room leading our discussion and answering questions. Somewhere, in the back of my mind, I decided I wanted to be just like one of them—the one who was also a "Debbie." She looked chic and beautiful, yet was so warm and friendly. And she seemed so confident! It made sense that I was drawn to her. I thought she had the answers I'd come to find.

My boys were eight and ten and I was there to learn how to keep a problem from starting in the first place: how to prevent drug abuse in the boys I loved—how to keep them safe from the unknown territory of the future. I was doing my best to learn all I could about giving my sons a foundation for a great life—and about how to protect them. I wanted to be a good parent—a really good parent.

In Parent-to-Parent I learned a story about navigating unknown territory. Maritime legend says that in days of old, as mapmakers drew their maps to guide sailors across the seas, they added a warning in the blank spaces beyond the bounds of the world they knew. They said, "Here be dragons." Although no one has yet found a map with those actual words on it, a copper globe from 1510 has them and a number of old maps do have drawings of dragons waiting in uncharted waters.

Maybe that image challenged me. I didn't want any dragons to get my kids—or any other kids I knew. Not only did I finish the class, I went on to become a Parent-to-Parent Trainer where I was awarded my own "Certificate of Dragon Slaying Proficiency." It says,

> *Be it known to all persons that the above named person...*
> *is qualified to train others in the fine art of dragon slaying.*

I don't think I ever became as chic and sophisticated as Debbie, but since then I've spent a lot of time training parents and teachers. Along the way I've learned a thing or two about dragon slaying. There can be a lot of dragons lurking in the unknown future, but dragon slaying is all about confronting the unknown with a plan. The trick is finding a plan that works. And that reminds me of another story about maps.

In 1513, a man named Admiral Piri Reis created a map of the known world for the Sultan of the Ottoman Empire. Only about a third of the map has survived, but what remains is a beautifully inscribed, gazelle-skin parchment colored in black and red. In crafting it, Reis said he'd relied upon twenty other, older maps. Some may have come from the Library of Alexandria, the fabled repository of the ancient world's knowledge. The piece that survives shows the coast of Brazil on the left and the coasts of Europe and North Africa on the right. Scholars generally agree that those depictions are fairly accurate. But there is a lot of controversy about what it shows at the bottom.

At the far south of the map, stretching across the bottom of the world, is an expanse of coastline that some believe is a match for the pre-Ice Age northern coast of Antarctica. The only problem is that Antarctica was not "discovered" until 1818—more than 300 years *after* Piri Reis drew his map—and it is now covered in ice over a mile deep. If the map does show Antarctica's northern coast, it had to have been surveyed and charted sometime before 4000 BC, which is the last time it was ice-free. And that would mean that ancient wisdom about the coast of Antarctica had been lost for centuries.

I tell that story because it reminds me that the wisdom of past generations—whether it is a map, a plan, or important knowledge—is sometimes "lost" as fads come and go, only to be found and then lost and found again. At the heart of what we teach in this book is ancient wisdom. From time to time it fades from sight, becomes popular for a while, and then fades again. Maybe one day it will become common knowledge, but for now, each generation has to learn it anew.

In fact, we'd already written this book when I happened to read a great book by the journalist Paul Tough called *How Children Succeed*. His reporting and writing focus on education, child development and poverty. In *How Children Succeed* he tells the story of new research that is revealing "new knowledge" about what creates successful outcomes in young lives. It was interesting and surprising to see that most of the "new" knowledge this research has uncovered is what drove the success of our summer camp in the Michigan wilderness sixty years ago and guided success seekers a hundred years before that. It still works today.

For your journey through the uncharted waters of the future, we have a plan—a formula—that will be your map. The Flying Eagle Formula is a 10-step approach to guide you. But it is so much more. When you follow the Flying Eagle Formula, you tap into wisdom of the ages that will equip a boy with the very essence of success. Our proof? Thousands of successful men who learned the lessons of the Flying Eagle Formula as boys. It just works.

Maybe you're like me—wanting to get it right and be a "good" parent. Or maybe you are haunted by the thought that we only have a short window of time to make a big impact on our kids. A friend told me he almost panicked when he realized he'd only have eighteen Christmases with his son before the boy left for college. Then he whittled that down to eight, reasoning that his son might only listen to him between the ages of five and thirteen. He's trying to make every one of those years count. I remember how that felt! Or maybe you want to do all of the things your parents or teachers did well, but somehow avoid all of their mistakes. Perhaps you want to protect the boys you love from drug abuse, bullying, gun violence and sexual exploitation. It seems that every day the news is filled with one horrible story after another that make us just want to *do* something. Or maybe you want to give your son every advantage and do all you can to equip him with the skills he'll need to navigate an unknown world ahead: the job market, relationships, and a lifetime of fast-paced change.

Whatever your motivation, this program will help your son and it will change you, too. I can pretty much guarantee that if you apply the lessons in this book you will become a better parent, a happier person, and that success will find you in ways you never expected.

A lot of books have been written about raising boys and most are very good. Some suggest doing some of the things that we outline here. But none of them deliver a program designed to create and harness the power of a success mindset the way this book does.

Why is The Flying Eagle Formula different? What is the ancient wisdom at its heart? Just this...

Who we believe we are, and who we decide to be,
determine our life.

Success comes to those who believe they are successful.

Confucius is thought to have said, "Those who think they can and those who think they can't are both usually right." However, we often don't even realize we've decided we can't. Those decisions are buried deep inside of us and may come from long ago. Yet they rise to the surface when we interact with children because how we see *ourselves* is how we see *them*. How we interact with children reflects what we believe about ourselves. The limitations we think we face influence the limitations we think they face. That's why having children can be so challenging. We come face to face with our past. Our children come to us as mirrors.

The amazingly successful Camp Flying Eagle program worked because it suspended judgment about who the boys were and what they were able to accomplish and allowed them to be and become who they chose to be. "Swim the lake before you row the boat" was a real part of camp life, but it is also a metaphor for the formula that transformed boys into confident young men.

And, while this book is about a summer camp, the truth shared here is about much more. Every spiritual path teaches it in one way or another. In the Bible, Jesus is quoted as saying, "If ye have faith as a mustard seed, you can move mountains." That faith isn't about size or how much faith one has. It isn't about how great you are in stature or how blessed your table may be. It's really about a deep sense of knowing who and what you are. A mustard seed doesn't question what it is. It simply is, and grows. If we know who we are, if we truly understand what beautiful beings we are, we can step into that same kind of knowledge.

The Flying Eagle Formula is a very practical way to share a sense of confidence in who our children are so that they can step into that state of *knowing* that they are successful, able to tackle new things and succeed, respected, liked; that their contribution is valued, that life is fun, that people like to be around them, that their opinion *counts*, that they are beautiful and complete and that, in a very fundamental way, *they matter*.

It's *that* sense of knowing that can move mountains.

It works because the human mind is *THE* most powerful force for shaping lives, destinies and the world. That's the message of books such as *The Law of Success* and *Think and Grow Rich*. As Napoleon Hill tells it, he was challenged by Andrew Carnegie, one of the richest men in the world, to interview the most successful men in America to learn the secret of their success. When he published *The Law of Success,* the law he revealed was this: "What the mind of man can conceive and believe, the mind of man can achieve."

Hill wrote *The Law of Success* in 1928, but even earlier, James Allen wrote *As a Man Thinketh* and said that our minds are like a garden. Whether you cultivate your garden or neglect your garden, you will end up with something, either a beautiful harvest or weeds.

We don't want weeds—for ourselves or our children. That means we have to consciously cultivate a beautiful garden. The possibility of cultivating our minds or harnessing the power of our minds to grow as a beautiful garden isn't new, but it *is* gathering new attention. Today's athletes use it to perfect performance through visualization. Olympians practice visualization right along with the physical part of their sport. Every swing, every stride, every move is choreographed in their minds ahead of time, all the way through to the award ceremony as they "hear" the national anthem play and see themselves step up on the podium to accept their medals. Many sports psychologists and performance coaches now teach that success is ninety percent mental and only ten percent physical. The idea of visualization is the basis for vision boards, affirmations and the sale of lottery tickets.

But we believe that there is even more to success than visualization. Have you heard the phrase, "the rich get richer"? Why do you think that is? Sure, they have a number of advantages. With money, they can buy more businesses and stock, and influencing legislation is certainly easier. But that's not the deciding factor. The fundamental reason that the rich get richer is because they think of themselves as rich. It isn't a goal—it is their *identity*.

That identity, that belief, that very embodiment of richness— they don't just visualize it, they ARE it. They become it. And it draws more of it to them. It's as if they make a home for richness and richness comes home to them—and the experience of being rich repeats and repeats.

In this book, we are applying those truths, those principles, to parenting. We are going to show you how to get the different characteristics of a success identity, that very embodiment of success, embedded within a child so that the experience of being successful comes home to him and repeats and repeats. A diagram of the formula we teach is on the next page.

At the bottom is the foundation, at the top the result. We are going to focus on the foundation: your WHY, WHAT you do, and WHAT he does. But the real secret is not found in what *you* do. The real secret to success is *what he thinks about himself*—from what he does and from what you do…and that can be entirely different from what you intended at the time. To get the results you really want, we will show you ten specific ways you can use our proven program to create success.

We learned these lessons from twenty-seven years of running Camp Flying Eagle. It only operated for a few weeks each summer,

THE FLYING EAGLE FORMULA

— THE RESULT —

Future experiences that
validate what you helped him
believe about himself

What he *believes*
about himself

What he
thinks

What
he *does*

What you do

Your WHY

— THE FOUNDATION —

but the experience of those weeks was so powerful, it continues to produce results. In this book, we'll walk you through a step-by-step process of *HOW* to get those results and deliver that lifetime advantage. If you are a teacher or work with boys, these lessons will show you how, in even just the short time you may have with them, you can embed a seed of success that will continue to grow for a lifetime.

This is the most important job you will ever have. I can tell you from experience, they grow up too fast and your window of time together will be all too short. Who will your child be if he grows up confident and self-assured, certain of his value, with great friends, loving relationships and looking forward to his future? What will that be like for you…to feel appreciated, loved and respected, with a son who looks forward to spending time with you, perhaps as a partner in your business, perhaps bringing grandchildren to visit, perhaps calling on the phone "just to talk"? What will it feel like to know you have done your best to give a boy the foundation for an amazing life?

We are going to help you find out. And somewhere along the way, you'll also come face-to-face with the truth about yourself. You, too, are beautiful, whole and complete. The challenges our children present are simply an opportunity to see that in both them and us.

Any one of us can follow this time-tested map to success…and in the next chapter, as you listen to Tess tell the story of how it all started, you'll see that you can, too.

Tess & Alex

CHAPTER TWO

THE JOURNEY FORWARD

A lex and I were probably a lot like you. We began with hopes and dreams, but I am not sure we had a plan. Our path simply unfolded until a point when our intention crystalized.

It started in 1945. I was sitting in class at the beginning of my second year of college at the University of Michigan. The girl next to me was crying. "I'll never speak to that Alex Canja again!" she sobbed.

I looked around. I didn't know "that Alex Canja," but I'd seen her with him. I worked at Goodyear's Snack Bar and they had come in for "Coke dates"—that meant talking over a Coca-Cola at the drugstore soda fountain. Handsome and athletic, he was one of the GIs who'd recently returned from World War II.

Where is that man? I wondered. *I'll give him a piece of my mind!* As it turned out, I didn't have to look too far to find him. The very next day, he walked out of the lecture hall next to me and asked if *I* wanted to join him for a Coke. Of course, I said *yes*, planning to find out just what he had done to make that girl cry.

And that's how it all started.

Looking back, it seems we were kind of mismatched. I grew up in the small village of Canajoharie in upstate New York. Canajoharie had only two thousand residents and it was easy to get your arms around life there. Everything was close. Families were close and friends were close. Both Mom and Dad worked close to home. If you went down the hill about three houses and turned the corner (there was a bakery there), you arrived at the sack factory where Mom worked making bags to hold flour and sugar. She walked to work and Dad walked to work, too, at the Hotel Wagner, which was also just down the hill. So was the grade school. My sister and I walked out the door, down the hill and just across a side street where a sheriff's deputy would direct traffic to get us across Route 10.

Growing up in Canajoharie was happy, warm and secure, a Norman Rockwell kind of life that was simple and sweet. A creek bubbled through town and we all had picnics at the swimming hole with our families. We stood under the Canajoharie Falls in our bathing suits and let the spray pour down on our heads. I remember milkmen delivering milk in winter with the cream frozen on top and rising out of the glass bottles, cars with running boards and rumble seats, roller skates that you tightened with keys, boxes of soap with dishes inside, three cent stamps, flexible brown records for Victrola machines that you played with a hand crank and popsicle sticks with "free" stamped on them—if you got one you could trade it in for another popsicle.

We danced to Big Band music and girls collected pictures of movie stars. The boys collected pictures of voluptuous movie star pin-ups. The number one song on the day I was born was *"Stardust"* and it was played at every school dance I ever attended. I was sure I'd come back to Canajoharie after college, get married and raise a family there.

But that's not what happened. When I was in high school, my English teacher left to work on her master's degree at the University of Michigan and then wrote to me. "Come to Michigan," she said. "Scholarships are available." I applied and received a scholarship and, in the fall of 1944, I boarded a midnight express train to Ann Arbor, Michigan. It was my first time away from home alone.

I still remember the thrill of that September day when I saw the university. The campus was huge, with at least twenty thousand students. That was ten times as large as my entire hometown! The trees were just beginning to turn brilliant fall colors and the buildings loomed large and grand. From the very beginning, I loved it!

I was assigned to live in a "League House," a residence converted to housing for women. On the third day of that first week in Ann Arbor, four of us gave each other nicknames. That's how I became "Tess." My real name is Esther (because I was born on Easter) and I don't know why they picked Tess, but it was as Tess that I met Alex.

Maybe our meeting was destined. The summer after I graduated from high school and before leaving for Ann Arbor, Mom and I took the train to New York to shop and visit her sisters and their families. In the city we stopped at a gypsy tea room and, just for the fun of it, had our tea leaves read. The gypsy reader told me, "There's an AC in your future." We laughed. I was dating Bob Fox at the time and who knew? After college, if we both still felt the same way about each other, we might get married. But by my sophomore year, Bob had become a distant memory.

Alex took a different path to college. It seems strange now, in a world of social media where we share so much about ourselves on Facebook and Twitter and where everything about our lives can be found on Google, but back in the 1940s, if you didn't grow up in the same town, you really only knew someone through what they told you, or what others told you about them or what you could see for yourself.

Alex rarely talked about himself, and he didn't talk about his family. Even to this day, I don't really know very much about his early life because that's the way he wanted it. I think he wanted to forget.

He was born in Flint, Michigan in 1921. His family included a younger sister, Gerri, and four older stepbrothers and a stepsister from his mother's first marriage. By his third birthday, his father was gone. Where or why, I don't know. When he was eleven, his mother returned to Hungary to take care of some sort of family issue, and she never returned. At that point, he must have felt like an orphan and maybe he was. Many years later, a letter written in Hungarian came for him, but I don't know what it said. He threw it away without trying to find out.

When his mother left in 1932, the country was in the middle of the Great Depression. Flint was hit hard and, at some point after the age of eleven, Alex's stepsiblings decided they could not afford to take care of him. He was sent to live at the YMCA.

The YMCA, the Young Men's Christian Association, started in England in 1844 when young men from the country came to the city for jobs. Street crime was everywhere and the first Y was organized to replace life on the street with prayer and Bible study. In the 1850s, the Y came to the United States with the same mission. By 1932, it had added dormitories, gyms and swimming pools and was focused on improving mind, body and spirit.

At the Flint Y, Alex learned to swim and dive. Diving is a sport of precision. Perhaps it taught him about self-control and discipline, or perhaps he brought control and discipline to diving. In any event, he needed it to survive. Life at the Y was not easy. He sold newspapers to support himself, earning only a penny for each paper sold. He once said he stood outside all day and made only three cents. He never talked about life at the Y or about his life growing up in Flint, but discipline and control surely helped him survive.

Through it all, he was driven to succeed, to excel, to prove him-self. He earned national recognition while diving for the Y team and was invited to join the University of Michigan swim team on a diving scholarship. It was the only possible way he could afford to go to college. He arrived in 1940 and that year the Olympics were cancelled because of World War II. Two years later, at the age of 21 and in the midst of his promising diving career, Alex was drafted. He joined the Army Air Corps as a signals operator using Morse code to send instructions to aid the pilots in the air.

Alex never talked about his service in World War II, perhaps because he landed on the beach at Normandy, France on the second day of the D-Day invasion and must have seen horrific things. As the GIs approached Omaha Beach, their landing craft hit sandbars and they were forced to wade through the water to reach the shore. They then had to make it across an open beach as they were gunned down by German soldiers. More than two thousand died. On the second day of the invasion, the dead bodies of GIs still lay on the beach and floated in the water. He never spoke of it. His sister, Gerri, died in childbirth while he was in the Army, and he didn't talk about that either.

Instead, every waking moment that he wasn't working outside or working at the office, Alex listened to music and sometimes sang along. He always had music playing in the background: Big Band sounds, Frank Sinatra, Andy Williams, Bing Crosby, Nat King Cole. He loved them all. I think that the words and the music filled his mind, lifted his spirit and kept the memories away. I think he wanted to forget.

So, in those days without the internet and Google, I only knew of Alex what he told me. On our first Coke date, he said he was a student at the university before he was drafted and now, as a returning soldier, he had the GI Bill that paid for his tuition and living expenses and gave him a chance to finish his education. He also said that he was working at the front desk of the Michigan Union. The Union was a U of M landmark, a big part of campus and the home of a campus-wide men's club. The Union was also where many of the BMOC (Big Men on Campus) had jobs. I didn't know any BMOC. I didn't even know what they were.

Unbelievably, Alex never told me he was on the swim team. In fact, he never talked much about himself at all. Instead, after a couple more Coke dates, he invited me to a swim meet. "I can't take you," he said, "but I'd really like to have you there."

It wasn't until I was actually at the pool that I learned he was a member of the team *and* a diver. I couldn't believe what I was seeing. He twisted and turned, backward and forward, doubled up and laid out, doing dives with names like "half, half, one-and-a-half." He was good. Very good. A three-time All-American.

I was also amazed to find out that in addition to working and going to school, he spent hours and hours every day practicing at the pool. I was impressed by his drive and his dedication. I began to spend more and more of my time at the pool watching him practice and compete at every swim meet. Soon a year had flown by in a mix of studying, working and swim meets.

One day, when I was working at the snack bar in my bright green dress uniform with its puffy sleeves and frilly white apron, Alex came rushing in, talked to my supervisor for a minute, grabbed my hand and pulled me out the door and down the street. "Quick! I have to show you something," he said. People turned to watch as we hurried by.

He walked me around to the back of a campus building and sat me down on a bench. It was my birthday, April 17, 1947. I had just turned twenty and Alex was twenty-five. He slowly reached into his pocket and pulled out a lovely gold ring with a topaz stone.

"Will you marry me?" he asked.

Would I? I said YES!

We married in a small ceremony and the next year we graduated and moved to Chicago for jobs. A year or two later we came back to the University of Michigan so that Alex could get a master's degree in English. He wanted to become a teacher. He wanted to provide the kind of adult guidance and mentoring that had been missing in his own life.

In 1948, we traveled to England with the U of M swim team for an exhibition tour. That's me in the front and Alex on the far right in his varsity sweater.

His first teaching job at Ypsilanti High School paid three thousand dollars a year. When he next moved on to Grosse Pointe High School to teach English and coach the swim team, his salary almost doubled to nearly six thousand! That was enough money to allow me to be a full-time mom to Debbie, born in 1954, and Jeff, born in 1956. We were even able to save two thousand dollars. It seemed like a fortune and I was looking forward to buying a new car.

It was Labor Day weekend in 1956 when I thought we'd found one. Alex was reading the *Detroit News* and he pointed to a small ad.

"Look! Look at this!" he said excitedly.

And there it was...an ad that would change our lives. It wasn't for a new car. Instead, a summer camp for boys was for sale.

I didn't know what to think. A summer camp? Neither of us had ever even seen a summer camp. No one had sent Alex to summer camp and I doubt my parents had ever heard of it. What was he thinking? While he had become a teacher and coach to make a difference in the lives of others, owning a summer camp seemed a huge leap beyond that!

Maybe the idea started at the many gatherings of U of M swimmers that we attended during the 1940s and early 1950s. Michigan's legendary swim coach, Matt Mann, owned a summer camp for boys, Camp Chikopi, in Magnetawan, Canada. Almost every other team member had either attended the camp or been a counselor there. When those swimmers got together, they talked about what they would do when they got their own camp, what they liked and what they would do differently. And now, here was a summer camp for sale on Crooked Lake in Northern Michigan.

Alex was really excited! Just minutes after seeing the ad, he called a friend. Two weeks later, they made the drive "Up North" to Kalkaska County, about fifty miles northeast of Traverse City.

Today "going Up North" is like a religious pilgrimage to a lot of folks who live in downstate Michigan and the states below, such as Ohio, Illinois and Indiana. I know people who live and spend nine months of the year talking about what they are going to do Up North during three months of summer.

Surrounded by four of the five Great Lakes, Michigan has three thousand miles of freshwater coastline, sixty-two thousand inland lakes, beautiful beaches, majestic sand dunes and quaint lakeside villages known for artist colonies, gourmet restaurants, wine and craft beer. Its west coast is called "the Caribbean of the North" because of the stunning colors of the water and the sugar-sand beaches. It's a vacation mecca.

But back in 1956, getting to that Up North paradise could be challenging. This was before the interstate highway system was built and before many roads were even paved in that part of the North Country. It took Alex and his friend John over six hours to make the drive. But it was worth it! He loved what he saw—a crystal clear lake surrounded by trees, sparkling in the sunshine with a sandy beach and acres of land to explore. Just two weeks later, I was headed Up North alongside Alex—with Debbie and Jeff lying on the back seat, in the days before seatbelts, surrounded by pillows, blankets and toys.

We arrived and I was awed by the sight: a lovely, soft, blue-green lake, glistening, sparkling in the sun, rippling on sandy shores. I agreed. It was beautiful.

And so our adventure began, and we set out to bring an idea to life.

Our philosophy

SUCCESS STARTS WITH THIS

H ave you ever had one of those moments when an idea sneaks into your mind and won't leave? That's what happened to us. A dream of actually owning and operating a summer camp began to take shape in our minds. For some reason we thought we could do it, and it was that thought that made all the difference. Even though we were naïve and had no real business savvy and no experience in operating a camp, we succeeded. And here's why.

If you've read Napoleon Hill's books or seen the movie *The Secret,* you know they teach that a key factor in creating what you want in your life is to write it down. The more specific you are, the better. That's the idea behind Franklin Covey planners—write down the goals you want to achieve and the steps you need to take to get there, and plan every day to include action on your plan.

In 1956 I hadn't read Napoleon Hill's book and Franklin Covey hadn't yet made planners, but I did write down our dream and the results we wanted to achieve. That's the first step to deliberately creating success, whether you are running a business or raising children. When you write down what your mind has conceived, you begin to believe and achievement follows. And so does attraction. Actually writing down our dream and committing it to paper helped to sharpen our goals, shape our actions, guide our decisions and attract opportunity. We always kept in front of us the vision we had of the outcomes we wanted to see.

Raising children can be a wild ride. Good support is important, but even more important is having everyone working from the same instruction page. Whether there are two of you or four of you, and especially if you are working with others, it is important to come to agreement on what you are trying to accomplish. When two or more are gathered in agreement, the combined intention is greater than the sum of the parts.

Conventional wisdom says it's businesses that need business plans and mission statements to keep everyone working toward common goals. I think it's wrong to limit that to business. I think we all need them to help us gain a clear vision of the role we will play in the lives of the children around us and to harness the power of our combined intention.

What result do you want? Think about it. If you are a parent, have you taken the time to actually describe what you hope will be the result of your parenting twenty years from now? If you are a teacher, what do you hope to give your students as a lasting result of spending time with you every day for nearly nine months or more?

For us, our camp philosophy kept us all working together in the same direction and toward the same purpose. It guided us as we met each day's responsibilities, and it gave us a road map through uncharted territory. We called it the Camp Flying Eagle (CFE) Vision. It described what we were trying to accomplish and made it possible for us to share it with others. It was our clear vision that helped us find the right people to join us in our effort. It became the filter that Alex used to recruit our counselors and it led us to the special couple who became lifelong friends and partners in our camp adventure.

When we first bought the camp, we lived in a large apartment complex and traded babysitting duties with our neighbors, Dick and Gloria Black. Dick was a high school basketball coach; Gloria was a busy school volunteer. One summer, about three years later, they were driving through northern Michigan on their way to Minneapolis when they suddenly decided to detour and visit us. It was a spur-of-the-moment decision. "We just showed up, and we really liked what we saw," Dick later said.

The very next year we needed a new Program Director and the rest is history. Alex and I worked side by side with Dick and Gloria for the next twenty-five years. Their entire family became as much a part of Camp Flying Eagle as ours. Gloria is still my best friend.

Have you ever heard it said that there are no chance meetings in life? Or that we can't possibly know all of the many ways in which a solution might appear, but by clearly stating our intention, by writing it down and envisioning the future, we attract that which we seek? It has happened that way to me in my life over and over. How else did Dick and Gloria come into our lives? They were, and are, just perfect. I know it was our clear vision that brought us together.

This is our vision statement and the philosophy we wrote down and shared with all of our staff. This is the "business plan" that made the difference:

The Camp Flying Eagle Philosophy:

We believe that young people today need success and a sense of accomplishment.

We believe they need opportunities to explore the world around them, to meet challenges, to appreciate their own capabilities and to find that they can do more than they thought they could.

We believe they need young friends and adult friends and an opportunity to develop positive interpersonal relationships at all age levels.

The Camp Flying Eagle Vision:

The goal of Flying Eagle is to provide an enriching experience in which each boy:

- ➤ recognizes his potential and abilities,
- ➤ develops skills that will provide lifelong enjoyment,
- ➤ learns to live cooperatively, sharing responsibilities,
- ➤ develops a love and respect for the natural environment, and
- ➤ achieves a sense of personal value and success.

We strive to ensure that each camper will:

- ➤ learn at least the basics of every major activity offered,
- ➤ have an opportunity to pursue special interests in at least three areas,
- ➤ be encouraged to develop/refine skills in at least three interest areas,
- ➤ develop competence and self-reliance in the water,
- ➤ develop an appreciation of the natural environment and Michigan lore,
- ➤ have an opportunity to plan and carry out a project that contributes to the fun, comfort or safety of other campers,
- ➤ improve in health and conditioning,
- ➤ be given many opportunities to succeed,
- ➤ expand his creative and linguistic abilities, and
- ➤ learn to participate as a member of a group, sharing responsibilities.

What are you trying to accomplish for the children in your life? Do you have a philosophy to guide your parenting or teaching? Do you have a vision, a dream of the result you hope to see? Have you ever tried to write it down? Let's do that.

It starts with a long-term goal, a vision of the future day when your child will graduate or leave school or home or move on to a new stage of life. What then? What skills does he need to have? What personal character traits do you hope he embodies? What does he need to know? *And why?*

This is where you need to take a minute or two, or even a week or more, to think about and actually visualize what you WANT the future to look like for your child. This is also the time to think about the kind of relationship you want to have with him when the future arrives. What does it look like? Will it be different from the relationship you had with your father or mother? This is another way of saying we start with the end in mind. To start with the end in mind means to be able to describe what that end looks like with all of its important details.

Other analysts have called this a strategic visioning process. When it comes to business, you could probably fill an entire library with the number of books written about why businesses need to set a vision to guide their actions. Thousands of consultants, coaches and entire firms make their living by helping businesses envision what future success looks like and how to get there. Why? *Because it works!*

To begin, start with a draft; it doesn't have to be perfect. In fact, it won't be. Then wait a few days, review it and revise it. Again and again, if you need to. Once you have revised it to your liking, share it with anyone else who will be contributing to the effort. We made it a point to share ours with all of our staff.

Every year, our counselors joined us for a week before the campers arrived to help us get the camp ready. That week also helped to get all of us ready to work together. On the night before opening day, we held a pre-opening-day meeting where Alex would hand out our Counselor's Manual with everything I'd taken the time to write down. "This is your guide," he'd tell them. "We've discussed it all this week. I discussed it with you in our interviews. Now I'd like you to turn to the Camp Flying Eagle Philosophy while I read it aloud. This philosophy underlies everything we do at Flying Eagle."

When I think back on those days, it seems that raising children and guiding them through adolescence should hardly be left to the young and inexperienced. When we are new parents, we barely know what we are doing! But by keeping in mind a vision of the result we want to see and a philosophy to guide us in getting there, we can know where we are going.

The key is to do it consciously. We all have a vision of the future, whether we know it or not. It comes from our past in the form of the memories we hold of good times and bad. That vision will produce a similar future, good or bad, unless we pay attention and deliberately turn our thoughts to a vision of the future we want to see.

Alex was determined to produce a future for campers that was different from his own past. He learned to swim and dive at the Y, but he also learned something else that he said was summed up by the poet William Henley in his poem, *Invictus*:

> *It matters not how strait the gate,*
> *How charged with punishment the scroll,*
> *I am the master of my fate;*
> *I am the captain of my soul!*

Those words kept Alex going through difficult times. He believed he had the power to shape his life and determine his own destiny.

That belief also became an important part of the Camp Flying Eagle Philosophy. He wanted young boys to know they had the power to determine the path of their own success.

We wrote down what we wanted our summer camp experience to do for our young campers and the result we wanted to see. Then we followed our vision. What is the result you want for the children you care about? Describe it specifically. What do you want them to experience and why? Write it down, and it will happen.

REMEMBER...

Your goal is to embed a success mindset, an identity of being a successful person, into a young mind. To do that you must start with a written plan, a description of the end result you wish to see. That is because, as Napoleon Hill found, the secret of success is a mental one—what the mind of man can conceive and believe, the mind of man can achieve. *YOU* must first conceive it and believe it.

CHAPTER THREE
ACTION STEPS

1. To create a vision of the end result you'd like to see, ask yourself...

    a. What are the personal qualities you value in people?

    b. Think of someone you admire for the way they live or lived their life. What made you admire them? What made them special?

    c. What are the qualities you want your son or student to exhibit as a teen, an adult, a husband, father, or community member?

    d. What kind of relationship do you want to have with your future son? Is it different from the relationship you had with your parents? If yes, in what way?

2. If people you influenced were speaking at your funeral, what would you like them to say about you, about the things you did for them or how you changed their lives? Are these qualities you want your son to have?

3. What is your own definition of success?

4. What is your philosophy of your role as a parent or a teacher? What would you say is the "job" of a parent or teacher?

5. Draft a mission statement to describe the role you will play to carry out your philosophy. You will probably change it later, and that's ok. In fact, after you finish this book, you may want to come back and review all you have written here and make changes.

At the Award Board making plans to earn new awards

THE MAGIC INGREDIENTS
Achievement & Recognition

When he was growing up, Alex did not always have a family to look to for support and encouragement or to keep him on track. But he did know something about motivation. "My childhood could have turned out so differently," he said. "I could have been on the streets. I could have been in trouble." What kept him moving in a positive direction through school was the self-confidence that came from experiencing success and the reinforcement that came from being recognized for his success.

That's how our camp vision began to work its magic. *The magic came because our written vision helped the adults understand their role*—especially the part about helping each boy recognize his potential and abilities *by experiencing success and a sense of accomplishment*. Motivating young children to try new things at which they might fail or trying to get them to keep working at a task they're not very good at can be hard. It can be even harder without a support structure of caring adults working together toward the same goals. But, once adults understand the end goal, the ways to get there will become clear.

For Alex, competitive diving was the path to success. Those who knew of his reputation as a swimmer and diver were surprised that our camp didn't specialize in swimming. But he knew that we all come with different strengths, interests and abilities, and he wanted every camper to enjoy recognition and success for his own unique talents and abilities.

That's why we began a never-ending effort to find and celebrate the "something" that each child could do successfully. Finding that "something" in each person and recognizing it is a key factor in fostering self-esteem, confidence and continued success. Our program was designed to find that something and embed a pattern of success in young minds, knowing that patterns created in childhood repeat themselves throughout our lives. As a result, we offered the broadest program we could, and we built in achievement and recognition whenever and wherever possible. It's never too early to start. Our campers ranged in age from seven to fourteen and some as young as six came with older brothers.

If, as Napoleon Hill, *The Secret,* and so many others have said, our thoughts create our reality, then the experience of success, the memory of success, and the emotion of success all change our way of thinking. Having experienced it once, our thoughts turn to the re-creation of success, to doing it again, to re-experiencing the thoughts and emotions that fill us when we succeed. You've heard the phrase "success begets success"? That's why. Our minds remember and *know* success and create more of it. By helping children experience success, we help them create a mental pattern of success.

We now know that our body and brain react equally to the visualization or mental imagining of a situation as they do to the actual event. That is why reliving a disaster or a bad experience over and over can have as powerful an effect as when it first happened. And that's why the opposite is also true. Reliving success brings more success. That is what is meant by bringing the past into the present and thereby creating the future.

Some call it the Law of Attraction. In his book, *The Nature of Personal Reality*, the author, Seth, says this: "What exists physically exists first in thought and feeling. There is no other rule... The world as you know it is a picture of your expectations." If that is so, we surely want to abandon our thoughts of bad experiences and instead relive and remember our thoughts of success. At Flying Eagle, it was our goal to make sure that each boy experienced success, felt it, *knew* it and remembered it.

While your own family or classroom or program will be unique, with its own opportunities for achievement, here are some ideas from what we did.

Creating Opportunities for Achievement

Although Alex was never a Boy Scout, he liked the Boy Scout system of award patches displayed on a sash. Every winter, I bought armloads of material and spent hours and hours cutting out and sewing together sashes of different sizes. Each year's sash was a different shade of green, gold or brown. We found a wonderful supplier of award patches and they began to design and make special ones for us. Over the years, we came up with over forty different awards to recognize accomplishment. Earning eight of those awards earned a Green Eagle award, sixteen earned a Gold Eagle and twenty-four, a Brown Eagle. Each winter I also cut out hundreds of eagles from green, gold and brown felt.

Because we were on a lake, no award brought more pride or was more coveted than the swimming award. In order to be allowed to go out in a boat by himself, or even with another camper, a boy had to be able to swim across the lake. Crooked Lake is not a big lake, but when you are out in the middle of it, the shore looks far away. From the shore, a person in the middle looks pretty tiny. Swimming the lake is a real accomplishment. When a boy knew he could swim the width of the lake, it meant that no matter where he was on it, if something happened, we knew, and *he knew*, that he could swim to shore. It gave him confidence in his abilities.

That rule became a challenge and an incentive. Everyone learned to swim. Norm, our waterfront director in the 1970s, told us, "My best memories were the looks of joy on the faces of campers the moment they realized they could actually swim." Not only did everyone learn to swim, just about everyone swam the lake. Some had to try it a few times, but eventually they all succeeded. Camper David told us,

> *Swimming the width of the lake was one of the first significant physical challenges in our young lives. It was our desire to earn the status of using the camp boats, but could we complete the swim? Not everyone made it across. So the first time you did, it was a memorable accomplishment.*

My three children all swam the lake by the age of seven. I can still remember how anxious I felt watching as my six-year-old son dog-paddled the entire way, his little head like a speck bobbing across a lake that looked enormous. Of course, Alex was swimming right beside him and a rowboat with life jackets was right there, too. From such experiences I learned to never, *ever* underestimate how capable young children are.

"Swim the lake before you row the boat" is how confidence becomes part of a success mindset. A boy might not have the skill in the beginning to swim across the lake or even the certainty he will make it, but by first deciding on his own that he wants to do it, then actually getting out there and trying, and finally succeeding, he *knows* himself to *be* a success. "Row the boat" is life. When you give young people a chance to swim a lake (meaning a challenging opportunity to accomplish something in an area where they *want* to succeed and they *can* succeed with your encouragement and support) you give them what they need to get in a boat and start rowing.

Swimming the lake was just the beginning of our campers' accomplishments and of our efforts to help them try more and accomplish more than they ever thought they could. Our camper Ross later told us:

> *CFE had a positive and permanent impact on my life. I learned and tried to do things that I might not have tried otherwise. It was the first time I tried waterskiing, riflery, archery, long-distance trip biking, karate, judo, boxing....*

In the earliest years, before we had many programs or much equipment, we found creative ways to challenge and reward the boys. These are things that can be done anywhere—no summer camp needed! The boys could earn an award for:

- ➤ playing three softball games, three football or basketball games (any game will do; three times ensures a certain mastery of it),
- ➤ hiking five miles,
- ➤ camping out overnight,
- ➤ completing three nature projects such as collecting and identifying leaves, stones or wildflowers,
- ➤ completing three craft projects,
- ➤ writing three stories for the camp newsletter.

We also had an award for catching three fish. Crooked Lake has a lot of fish in it and the fishing award was a nice oval patch with a picture of a big fish jumping out of the water with a lure in its mouth. To earn the award, a camper had to catch three "keepers," which meant a fish at least seven inches long. While the picture on the patch was the dream, the reality was more often a little perch or bluegill caught on a hook with a worm. We called those fish "bait stealers." A few campers caught larger fish like bass.

One year, one lucky camper hooked a really big one. Down went the pole, bending into the water as the fish pulled back. The young camper battled on, encouraged by a growing throng of campers and counselors. After a long fight, he finally pulled the fish out of the water. To the cheers of the onlookers, he marched it proudly up the beach, up the steps and into the Chow Hall, followed by his many admirers. Our cook Kay took one look at his catch and assured him that she could clean it and cook it for his dinner that night. She did, and as I came to help with the cooking that afternoon, I remember asking, "What IS that?"

"Why," she said laughing, "that's a seaweed fish!" And there it was, a beautifully prepared dish of lake weeds, hooked and pulled from the lake bottom. Our little camper got the last laugh, though. His seaweed fish counted toward his fishing award.

Through the National Archery Association, the boys advanced from Yeoman to Archer. Each new rank came with a pin or a patch for their sash. Through the National Rifle Association, they earned pins and patches from Pro-Marksman to Expert. A bullseye earned a pop (what we in Michigan call a soda) and bragging rights.

If a counselor had a special ability or interest that could be shared with the boys, we encouraged it. When Gloria became certified by the state as a camp health director, we added a first-aid award. Counselor "Mike the Bike" started long-distance bike trips. Any special skill, ability or interest presented another opportunity for sharing and for the boys to acquire a skill and to experience achievement in a new area. Have you taken the time to share skills you have or some special knowledge you hold with the children around you? What about family members? *Everyone* has something unique to share.

Most important, the boys were setting goals for themselves, working to achieve them and experiencing success. We created a big bulletin board to display all of the available awards so the boys could easily check it on their way to the beach or to the Chow Hall to eat. There were always boys standing in front of the board, looking to see which awards they wanted to earn next. They were learning that it's amazing what you can do when you set your mind to it.

The Importance of Recognition

Providing opportunities for children to achieve is only half the strategy. Achievement is always more special when it is accompanied by recognition. And why not? Sometimes I think that in our own families we withhold recognition and even celebration because we are saving it for "the big things" or "the most meaningful" accomplishments or the things that we, as parents, feel better about encouraging because of what we think it says about us. I've heard the concern that we can't let children come to expect a reward for everything they do. I agree. But when you have carefully thought about what you want to help encourage and why, recognition and celebration are powerful motivators. We could all benefit from receiving a little more positive recognition and celebration, couldn't we? I can also tell you from personal experience that the joy of giving recognition is just as great as the joy of receiving it.

A special newsletter sent to family and friends is a great way to recognize accomplishments. We started a camp newspaper, *The Eagle's Eyeful*. Now, *that* was a labor of love. Back in the day, before computers, it was produced on a type of tabletop printing press known as a "ditto machine." The machine had a metal drum and a handle on the side that you cranked to turn the drum. It used special, two-ply paper to create a "spirit master." When you typed or drew on the top sheet, it imprinted carbon ink on the second sheet. That second sheet was then wrapped around the drum and the drum was hand-cranked. With each complete turn, out came one copy! When the ditto machine was working well, we could crank out fifteen to thirty copies per minute. I'll never forget the rhythmic sound of cranking out hundreds of pages on the ditto machine as well as the unique smell of the liquid ink and the purple stain it left on your hands. But it was all worth it for the recognition campers received from seeing their name in print.

The Eyeful began carrying an "It's Amazing" column written by campers. It was a great way to recognize achievement publicly, and the achievement didn't have to be a "big" one to be recognized. When a camper was proud of an accomplishment, we recognized it. One long-time camper wrote this story:

TODD—earned highest award of the Camp Archery Association

SCOTT—earned the first Gold Fish Award for swimming the lake 15 mornings in a row

JASON—learned a front flip on the trampoline

ADAM—waterskied for the first time

CRAIG—earned 33 awards

BOBBY—caught a bass

ANDY—got a hit to third base

JEFF—got my tennis award

DREW—got a yellow belt in judo

GLENN—biked 110 miles

JOSE—made three scores in soccer

TY—found the most Petoskey stones (150)

MATT and MARC—read the most books in camp

The Importance of Celebration and Ceremony

Recognition can take many forms, but one thing we were sure of: recognition is always more special when it is accompanied by some sort of ceremony. You have only to look at the many public award ceremonies for adults that dominate the news to know that awards given during a ceremony have impact, signify a special success and are remembered. That's why every Friday night, about an hour or so after dinner, the campers lined up in front of the Chow Hall. There they received the sashes I had stitched together over the winter months, with their names inside. If it was the first Friday night of the camp session, the sashes would be bare, but they didn't stay that way for long because this was Council Fire night, a tradition we took from Native American lore. Alex always felt it important to honor the Native Americans who walked the land before us. Our campers were divided into tribes with names like Iroquois and Comanche. The Council Fire was a time when the tribes gathered together.

It was the ceremony of the Council Fire that made it special and gave it impact. That ceremony started long before the campers ever reached the clearing in the woods where it was held. The camp bell would ring, campers would gather and, at the appointed time, walk single file in silence across our long, grassy baseball field to the edge of center field, where a path was lit with tall, burning torches and led into the woods. Walking in silence helped to impress upon them the significance of the ceremony. The burning torches signified that they were entering a place of importance. Counselors stood at attention on either side of the path, staring straight ahead with their arms crossed. Campers marched down the path to the beat of a loud drum and made their way to rows of wooden benches in the forest.

The Council Fire was a huge bonfire built on a raised platform. The oldest campers were responsible for building the fire and had the honor of lighting it. In seconds, the flames would roar toward the night sky and warm the faces of the campers sitting on the benches before it began to die down as the sun set. In the glow of the fire, each counselor stood before the campers and said a few words about achievement before he handed out the awards from his area. Campers were called up to receive awards and handshakes and to bask in the glow of recognition. Each boy was called up several times every Friday night.

After the ceremony, campers took off their sashes and carefully rolled up their awards inside so they could be brought to the Main Lodge where Gloria and I waited with our sewing machines. Every Friday night after Council Fire, Gloria and I sewed all of the awards on all of the sashes, no matter how long it took. One night we didn't finish sewing until 2:00 a.m.!

We insisted on finishing that night because, even though the next Council Fire was still a week away, just as important as sewing on the awards, and perhaps more important, we counted the awards as we sewed them on. If a camper seemed to be falling short of earning awards, we would think about his strengths and a plan of action was hatched to help him find new areas to conquer. I can't stress enough how important it was to us that every boy experienced success. It wasn't handed to them, they had to earn it, but we offered opportunities tailored to their individual strengths and abilities. Every Friday night's Council Fire was another opportunity for celebration.

If we didn't have an award patch for it, we found another way to create and recognize achievement. We began sending campers home with jars of jam that they helped make from the berries they had picked. Blueberries were so plentiful around the camp that I started making jam when I was in the kitchen on the cook's day off. As boys brought in the berries, I asked, "Would you like to make jam to take home with you?" Yes, they would, and that's how it happened that I had the company of young boys in the kitchen, scrubbing their hands clean, removing stems and leaves, washing and mashing blueberries, and making labels for jars of jam they could proudly take home as gifts for their families.

Another source of pride and recognition arose unexpectedly. Some of our younger campers, out with a counselor exploring a nearby lake, came upon an old campsite, possibly a logging camp from the 1800s. Their collection of treasures included a lot of old glass bottles with dirt inside and out. Their biggest prize? A large, iron frying pan with most of the bottom rusted out. It was not exactly a decorator piece, but we nailed that frying pan to the wall of our Main Lodge, lined up the dirty bottles and started a museum. The boys were so proud.

The award system, Council Fire, the *Eagle's Eyeful* and other forms of recognition and celebration did everything we hoped for and more. They encouraged the boys to try new experiences. They had the powerful effect of saying *"Well done"* and *"You can do it."* They created positive memories of success.

Is there a child in your life with interests or talents you can encourage? Are there accomplishments you can celebrate? Do you have a special talent or interest you can share? You don't need a lot of resources to recognize achievement and the recognition doesn't have to be elaborate, but ceremony helps. I encourage you to create a future of success by helping your children experience it now.

REMEMBER...

Keep in mind that your goal is for your son or student to really believe and *know* that he is a successful person. This is not something that you can simply tell him. He has to experience it. Your job is to introduce him to opportunities that will lead to those experiences or to create the opportunities. This does not have anything to do with competition or being better or more talented than others. You want him to come to *know*, through successful experiences, that he can tackle something new and succeed at it.

CHAPTER FOUR

ACTION STEPS

1. Think carefully about your son's strengths.

2. What are his likes and dislikes?

3. What opportunities for accomplishment can you provide that fit his strengths and/or interests?

4. Reread the list in the "It's Amazing" story from the Eagle's Eyeful in this chapter. The accomplishments were not necessarily "big," but they were important to the boy. Take a minute to brainstorm and make a list of the different things the boys in your life are trying to accomplish.

5. What are the different ways you could celebrate or recognize their accomplishments and success?

_____
_____
_____
_____
_____
_____
_____
_____
_____
_____
_____
_____
_____
_____

I first came to camp as a ten-year-old and was a camper for five years and then a Kitchen Boy. For me, the whole Camp Flying Eagle experience was about trying new things in a fun and safe environment so I could figure out who I was and who I wasn't. Today, I am a happy husband, father of two, and a robotics engineer. And 37 years after my last summer at CFE, I've still got all of my sashes and trophies carefully tucked away. I've taken them out to share with my children and I've tried to give them the experiences I had.

Todd (1977–1982)

Becoming a team

CHAPTER FIVE

BUILD A STRONG FOUNDATION

E ach year it took teamwork to get our camp ready for summer. Our huge baseball field had to be mowed, and the archery and rifle ranges had to be repaired after a long winter of being buried under the snow. The dock had to be carried out into the water, section by section. The dormitory where younger campers slept had to be cleaned and beds readied. The older campers slept in five big Army tents that surrounded the baseball field. Those had to be set up with their bunk beds and shelving moved in.

We also did *a lot* of painting to keep the camp looking fresh and new. Alex used to say that he learned two things in the Army—if it moves, salute it, and if it doesn't, paint it. The painting part of Army life was definitely part of our Camp Flying Eagle experience! But when everything was done, we viewed the results together with a shared sense of pride in our accomplishment.

Shared pride builds camaraderie, a feeling of belonging and of self-esteem. Each year, it proved that working together side by side to accomplish a goal multiplies joy. I have always found that lasting and satisfying happiness comes when two or more people work together to get something done. Being part of a team and contributing to a team effort enriches us. It is especially satisfying when you can see the difference you've made and know that your contribution mattered. It reinforces, in a memorable and meaningful way, that *you* matter.

Make no mistake about the importance of this. When our participation is needed and wanted and our effort is important to the success of the whole, we know we have a purpose and a place. *"I was needed,"* we can say. *"I was important to the outcome."* We all need to feel that we have a purpose and a place and a way to contribute.

Important, too, when we work together with others, they notice our contribution and we notice theirs. Perhaps, in an ideal world, we would all toil unselfishly and unnoticed, fulfilled by the knowledge that our work is important. But in the world I know, it is so much more joyous when friends, family and co-workers notice and acknowledge our work and appreciate our efforts.

That is why, after a long week of hard work and preparing for opening day, we always took time to celebrate together with a Friday night steak fry. It wasn't elaborate. We held the steak fry at the edge of the baseball field. We sat on folding chairs in the shade of a large tree or on a bench in the nearby dugout. The "grill" was a long, double line of cement blocks placed on the sandy ground about a foot apart with charcoal briquettes in between and grills from the kitchen ovens laid on top.

Alex was our Grill Master. In my mind, I can still see him, bending over the steaks, long fork in hand, with the smoke curling up from the coals, taking orders and rewarding each counselor, staff member and special guest with a steak cooked just the way it was ordered. I remember enjoying those steaks at the end of a long, hot day in early June, sitting in the shade with the breeze blowing across the baseball field and ruffling the leaves of the birch trees all around. It was a reward for a job well done, shared with a team.

The memory of having a purpose and place, the feeling of belonging that comes with being part of a team, and the feeling of self-worth realized when others value our contribution, are powerful motivators of adults and powerful teachers of children. By providing that experience, we help young children create a mental and emotional picture of being needed, of having something important to share, of feeling valued and of succeeding. That picture will draw more of the same to itself and create a future like the past they remember.

The lonely ones are those who see no function in the world for them to fill, no place where they are needed. Loneliness is a killer, the silent enemy. It can lead to depression, escape into alcohol and drugs and suicide. "Lonely-proof" your child. Recognize the importance of teamwork and contribution and commit to finding opportunities for your child to experience them.

This is as important to the child who is seemingly gifted or talented in a certain area as the one who isn't. The one who is not learns that his efforts *do* make a difference and that he *can* contribute and succeed. The one who *is* learns that not only have his efforts on behalf of the team made a difference, but that just as important to "winning" is the contribution of each and every member. Recognizing the power of teamwork is one of the greatest assets of a success mindset. After all, as any wise person will tell you, no one "does it alone." We all achieve success, in one way or another, with the help of others.

Teamwork, Camaraderie and Purpose

Teamwork, camaraderie and purpose were a deliberate part of our camp experience. As the camp season unfolded, we made sure that the boys experienced the joy of team accomplishment and team celebration. Many awards could only be earned by a cabin working together as a group. The Cleanliness award required an entire cabin to "pass inspection" every single day for a full week. The inspecting started as soon as the morning after arrival. Imagine a cabin full of nine-year-old boys who might not know each other, pulling together to make their beds with hospital corners, fold all of their clothes and place them neatly on shelves, sweep the floor and stand at attention while Alex or Dick prowled through the cabin looking for something out of place. And did I mention that the boys had to be clean, too? After about a week of camp activities in an all-male environment, that alone was an accomplishment.

"We were tough," said Dick. "We were especially tough with the older campers in the tents. We wanted them to understand what we meant by neat and clean and picking up after yourself. In the dorm, the counselors were allowed to help by giving advice, but the boys had to do the work. They learned to work together and to be responsible not only for themselves, but for each other."

A perfect score at inspection was a 10. One week of 10s earned each camper in the cabin the Cleanliness patch. Two weeks of 10s earned the Honor Cabin patch. Entire cabins waited in eager anticipation for Friday night's Council Fire when their accomplishment would be recognized in front of the entire camp.

Years later, however, we learned that boys can bring their own unique interpretation to cleanliness. One camper told us how proud he was as a ten-year-old when he figured out how to get four days of cleanliness out of each T-shirt: "Right side out and frontward, right side out and backward, inside out frontward and inside out backward!"

The Campfire award was earned on a Thursday night, the cook's night off, when cabins would collect a bag of dinner food from the camp kitchen and hike off to a special spot to build a fire and figure out how to cook it. Do you have a grill? Learning how to cook a meal for the family on the grill might not seem like a big deal, but it is a skill and learning to do as part of a team leads to an important sense of belonging and purpose.

The Overnight award was earned by going out as a cabin group on an overnight campout and sleeping under the stars, or maybe in a tent in the woods where stories were told around the campfire, and marshmallows for S'mores were roasted on sticks sharpened with a jackknife.

Team sports were a big part of Flying Eagle activities. We played enough baseball, softball, soccer and basketball to be competitive, and we sometimes played against other camps, most often Camp Tanuga or Camp Sancta Maria, both larger than Flying Eagle. "I will always remember the softball game we played against Camp Tanuga," said Bob, a camper from 1959–1962. "I was pitching, and Coach Black was impressed. But he was really impressed with my home run because no one could find the ball in the trees. Given my slow base speed, it was the only chance I had to make it around the bases and score a run!" Imagine. Fifty years later, he has not forgotten his contribution to the team.

Competitive sports do involve winning and losing, and while winning as a team is exciting, sometimes the real learning comes after a loss. "I used to tell my boys to always give it their best," said Dick, who for many years was a much beloved high-school basketball coach. "But let's face it," he added, "sometimes they give their best and the other team wins. Sometimes the other team is just better."

"I'd tell them," he continued, hunching forward in his chair, remembering, "to appreciate good playing. We'd analyze the game and if there were changes we could make to improve, we'd do it. The best workouts we ever had were after we lost a game. Those boys would be very determined to pull together and win the next one."

Being part of a team that is working together to learn, grow and accomplish is one of life's great satisfactions, and we quickly learned to seize every opportunity to offer it. For instance, in the summer, with the sailboats, rowboats and canoes out on the lake, the boathouse that sat at the edge of the lake became a dormitory for the Kitchen Boys, or KBs, who cleaned up the kitchen after every meal. One year, the water level of the lake rose so high it flooded the land between the boathouse and the kitchen. A counselor said, "If you will provide the materials, my campers would like to build a bridge to the boathouse."

What a great opportunity to work together, build confidence and develop skills! What a great chance to experience the satisfaction of making a lasting contribution that would be appreciated by others for years to come! The bridge built by those thirteen-year-olds was so sturdy it lasted twenty years. We recognized their contribution with a new and special award, a gold felt Service star.

Another year, our nature counselor told us his campers wanted to design and build a "nature hut," a roofed structure with a counter and cages underneath to hold snakes, turtles and other creatures they could catch to study and then turn loose. Campers did the planning and building. That structure, too, stood for over twenty years.

In 1969, a story appeared in the *Eagle's Eyeful*:

You Can Help Build the New Camp Store!

Campers who are interested in getting a Service award can help build the new camp store. It will be built in the circle of trees between the dorm and the bulletin board. After it's built, there will be a contest to name it.

Camper Mike added an update in the *Eyeful* later that summer:

Camp Store Nearly Finished!

Camp Flying Eagle has finally started a candy store. It's 7 feet high and 5 feet wide. If you want your Service award, you can help build it. The camper with the best name for it gets a prize.

We held a contest, and the winning name for the new camp store was "The Sugar Shack." Campers could buy flashlights, batteries, bug spray, pencils, camp T-shirts and sweatshirts at the Sugar Shack. But most important? They could also buy candy... with a catch. Before a camper could get his hands on even one candy bar, he had to show he'd written a letter home. No letter home, no candy bar.

The Sugar Shack still stands, now at our cottage across the lake. It is a testament to the teamwork that built it and the accomplishment of getting hundreds of young boys to write letters home. But again, we later learned how clever boys can be. More than one family opened up an envelope only to find the "letter" was a blank piece of paper!

Is there a project at your house or at your school or in your community that needs to be done? Is there something that needs to be fixed? Can you take the time to include the children you love in the effort? Even everyday tasks like doing the laundry can turn into "team" events. The little time and effort you take now will reap future rewards far beyond what you can imagine. If you have carefully thought through the vision of the results you want, it will guide you in the best way to use opportunities as they arise or will guide you to create them.

From Competition To Life Lessons

One of the biggest opportunities we created to promote teamwork came just once each summer. It was a two-day event called "Color War" because we divided the camp into two competing teams, the Brown and the Gold, our main camp colors. The events of Color War involved competition in all sports, including basketball, softball, soccer, archery and riflery. But Color War was about much more than competition.

The goals of Color War were carefully thought out and lofty: camaraderie, teamwork, inclusion regardless of ability, good sportsmanship, the desire to give an all-out effort and the satisfaction that, win or lose, the effort had been grand. The goals were so important that Alex, Dick and the counselors spent hours planning it, including how to announce it, how to divide the camp into evenly matched teams and how to carry out the actual events.

It was very important that the teams be evenly matched. President Kennedy once said how hard it is, in military or personal life, to ensure equality. He said, "Life is unfair." But wherever and whenever we had an opportunity to give every boy an equal chance, we did. This was especially true during Color War.

If an exceptional athlete was added to one team, an exceptional athlete would be added to the other. If a good archer was on one team, the other team would get one, too. If that was not possible, the other team would be given some other advantage such as the best marksman at the rifle range. The younger dormers competed against other dormers, and those in tents competed against others from the tents. Whatever their age, the boys knew they were up against fair competition. They knew their best efforts were needed and that all of them had to pull together. Wouldn't we love to work with people who felt that way?

And the reward? Color War winners got ALL the ice cream they could eat! The losing team had to be satisfied with just one bowl each. The ice cream record was held by Bob, who somehow managed to eat nine bowlfuls.

We did everything we could to make Color War memorable and special, including the surprise announcement heralding its start. We never announced it the same way twice, and the summer was filled with endless speculation about when and how it might begin. When the announcement finally came, the excitement could be felt throughout the camp!

For one of our first announcements, we woke the campers at 4:00 a.m. to tell them that a bad storm was on the way and that, for safety, they all needed to move to the Chow Hall. But once they were there, we gave them hot chocolate and announced that Color War had begun! Another night, we took the campers to a movie in a near-by town where, in the pre-movie announcements, the words "Color War Begins at Camp Flying Eagle" flashed on the big screen.

Another year, when the boys were on their bunks with their radios tuned to a local station waiting for an important news update, an announcer with a loud, urgent voice broke in. "Color War will begin at Camp Flying Eagle at three o'clock this afternoon!" Then there was the day a sheriff's car, with sirens blaring, drove into camp and an officer stepped out to announce, "Color War Begins!"

Of course, the announcements didn't always go as planned. One year we dropped leaflets from an airplane. They were supposed to land on the baseball field during a game, but the wind carried them off to the side where they fluttered down into the water. Another time, our waterfront director rode in on a horse. He was supposed to throw a spear into the sand and announce, "The Color War has started!" Though he'd said he knew how to ride a horse in his employment application, it turned out he didn't. He'd just put down "yes," thinking he could learn later. That day on the horse, he sort of hung on for dear life as the horse pranced around. But the boys knew what was coming.

The mission and purpose of Color War always guided us. Each Color War team selected its own captain and when we saw that it was usually an older camper from the tents selected, we had the teams select co-captains, with one from the dorm and one from the tents, so the contribution of the younger campers would be given the same importance. Cabin inspections were more difficult than the usual daily inspections. Teams lost points if the cleanliness of a team member did not measure up to the high Color War standards.

Peer pressure to wash up is a beautiful thing to behold in a group of boys.

The teams were so evenly matched that the outcome always came down to a final relay race, a marathon around the lake that involved running, swimming, boating and canoeing, with a baton handed off from person to person. The marathons were as exciting as any sporting event I have ever watched!

The *Eagle's Eyeful* reported the excitement:

One of the Best Color Wars EVER!

In one of the most exciting and dramatic Color Wars in Flying Eagle history, the Brown Team, captained by Tom, came through with a total of 621 points to the Gold team's 573!

The lead for first place swayed back and forth throughout the day and a half of competition. As the time for the Indian Marathon arrived, fewer than five points separated the Brown and Gold Teams.

The Marathon time for the Brown Team was 35 minutes flat! The Gold Team runner crossed the finish line just 45 seconds later.

An interesting sideline to the Marathon was the entry of a "dark horse" team, the "Kitchen Boys Four" who finished approximately one minute ahead of the Brown Team. The Kitchen Boys' baton was a wooden spoon with a pink bow, donated by the cook. In the opinion of the officials and the counselors, this was one of the best Color Wars ever, and every camper did his best in a sportsmanlike manner.

"I will never forget the Color War," a long-time camper wrote. "Win or lose, it was a great time."

Indeed, it was. The bonding across cabin lines, the cheering, the exhilaration, the satisfaction of giving it your all as a team, the suspense as every year the two days of competition came down to the running of the marathon, the sheer joy of victory and, even in defeat, the thought that next year was yet another opportunity to get *all the ice cream you could eat*—all created powerful feelings of belonging and the knowledge that success is within reach when you give your best effort and work together as a team.

Does every opportunity to contribute have to be as grand? No, it doesn't. I will never forget a story daughter Debbie told me. While in the supermarket, she noticed a toddler sitting in a shopping cart looking proud and happy. It was clear she had an important role to play in the shopping trip. She was needed. Why? Her job was to hold a cabbage. What a great idea! Even if she dropped it, a dropped cabbage is a small price to pay for instilling a sense of importance and contribution. "I wish I'd understood how necessary it was to find ways for my own kids to participate as part of the 'family team' when they were small," she said. "I was so busy trying to work full time and take care of the house that it seemed easier to do everything myself." While that approach might be easier, it won't help plant the seeds of future success in a child.

What sense of belonging and contribution can you instill in the children around you? Take time to really think about it. Can you ask others to join you and your child in a project and thereby create a team? Can you take on a task that helps others? Visiting seniors in assisted living, doing craft activities with folks in memory care, serving food at a soup kitchen, collecting toys or books for homeless kids, doing yard work for a disabled neighbor can all give a child the powerful message that he can make a difference, that his life has meaning and that his efforts are appreciated. Is there a project in your community that needs volunteers? Can you help your child contribute to team success? The benefits are worth every effort.

REMEMBER...

Your goal is to embed a feeling and belief of *belonging*. You want your son to know that *his contribution matters*. You want him to know that there is a purpose and reason for him to be here—that he *can* make a difference—that he *does* make a difference and that his value to the whole is known.

CHAPTER FIVE

ACTION STEPS

1. Think first about your family or classroom activities. Even if you don't "need" help, keep in mind the importance of your overall goal. What job can you ask your son to do, that you will NOT redo, that can stand as a contribution to the family? What can you ask your son or student to do together with you? Your goal is to create a sense of being part of a team working together.

2. Think next about your community. What activity can you both join in to make a difference in the lives of others?

3. Are there team activities he can join? Sports? Science Olympiad? Band, orchestra, robotics? This can be tricky because many competitive team situations can produce the opposite of your goal if not managed or coached with insight. Be careful to whom you entrust your child. Lifelong lessons are learned here—both good and bad.

Formation in front of the Main Lodge and Chow Hall

ENSURE GOOD BEHAVIOR

I remember one time toward the end of the opening day of our second session of the summer. The new campers had all arrived. The campers who had enjoyed the first session and were staying for the second had been sent to Traverse City for a day of "3Ms": miniature golf, McDonald's and a movie. Their bus had just returned to the camp and I was headed out to the parking lot to greet them. One of our new parents was just leaving and we walked together toward her car. We were talking in the parking lot when a boy hopped down from the 3M bus and she gasped.

"He's a camper here? If I had known that..." she said. She didn't finish the sentence, but it was obvious that, had she known, she would not have sent her son to Flying Eagle.

"Is something wrong?" I asked.

"He's a terror!" she replied. "He lives in our neighborhood, and he's always in trouble!"

I was astounded. "He's been an excellent camper," I told her. "One of our best. He even exhibits leadership qualities."

I remember her standing there shaking her head. As it turned out, both boys went on to have productive and happy stays with us. Over the years I've recalled that encounter and wondered what it was about the Flying Eagle environment that had made such a difference for the boy she pointed out. I believe it was our structure, routine and rules.

Structure and Routine Help Build Self-Esteem

My definition of structure is "an ordered way of doing something" and routine is the repetition of that order. Dick called it "consistency." There was no question about how the boys were expected to act, or what was appropriate conduct and what was not. There were no surprises about the kind of behavior we expected from our campers, what they were supposed to do and when.

Channeling the high energy of boys into achieving, growing and maturing team players is a lot easier when done within a structure and with a routine. Young children are eager to learn the rules and to play by them, as long as the rules are fair and they know what they are. Structure and routine provide the common rulebooks for them to follow. At camp, when we provided structure and routine, good behavior blossomed.

If your own schedule impacts the young people around you and you would like good behavior to blossom, consider this. When you come right down to it, structure and routine help build self-esteem. Think about how frustrating it is when you can't figure out what it is you need to do to please your boss, your teacher, your parents, your friend or your spouse. What are the expectations and rules, you wonder. Not knowing creates stress and anxiety. On the other hand, when we know what is coming next, we can adjust our behavior to fit in. When we fit in, we feel we belong. When we feel we belong, we feel better about ourselves and about others. The need to belong is so powerful that it changes behavior. Who among us hasn't changed our behavior in an effort to better fit into a group?

Our camp routine and structure took away the anxiety of uncertainty, freeing the boys to focus on learning new skills and succeeding. Your own schedule has the potential to do the same, *but only if everyone touched by it knows what it is **ahead of time***. In the world of education, the structure and routine would be in the class syllabus and the class schedule. At Camp Flying Eagle, the structure and the routine were in the daily program.

The Camp Flying Eagle Daily Program

Because Alex and Dick had been in the military, they borrowed from military traditions. Our daily program followed the same schedule Monday through Friday. Sticking to an exact schedule helped the boys anticipate and conform their behavior to the program's expectations. Our daily schedule *always* started *every* morning at 7:20 with Alex and Dick walking through the camp cheerfully yelling this wake-up call:

All right! All right! ALL RIGHT!
Ev-ery-body UP!
It's another GREAT day at Flying Eagle!

Creating a special and happy way you can greet the young people in your life every morning is easy to do. Greeting every child at breakfast or at the classroom door with "Good Morning, Sunshine!" can go a long way toward creating a sunny day. It anchors the day with a sense of familiarity and routine.

Ten minutes later, the campers and counselors were out on the baseball field for "cals," a brief session of calisthenics that included pink-bellies (toe touches with a slap on the belly on the way up and another on the way down), jumping jacks and stretches. Instead of cals, campers could choose to go for a morning polar bear swim in the lake or jog with a counselor. Those options were always announced the night before in order to let campers know what to expect so that they could learn to plan ahead. Knowing what is coming next is a critical component in learning to take responsibility for planning ahead.

At the end of each day, can you take time to review the next day's activities, both for yourself and for the children in your life, to help them plan ahead and to foster and encourage their desire to behave and fit in?

Formation

Before every meal, our campers stood together in cabin groups on a large cement patio in front of the Chow Hall in a ceremony known as Formation. A flagpole anchored one end of the patio directly across from the door that kept ravenous campers from storming the dining room before the food was ready. No one wanted to be late or missing from Formation because it meant your cabin would be the last one dismissed into the Chow Hall for the meal. Food is a huge motivator of young boys. I'm convinced that the chance to be first in the door motivated more than a few to change their shirts, wash their hands and show up on time.

"AT-TEN-TION!" With that command, Alex would call the camp to order and campers and counselors would stand at attention. Alex would turn to each cabin and say, "Ottawa, report!" or "Chippewa, report!" to get an attendance report from each cabin. One by one, a selected camper from each cabin would step out and report to Alex or Dick: "All present and all accounted for, *Sir!*" and salute. Alex or Dick would salute back and say, "Thank you!" It was a ritual of respect and order.

At least it was supposed to be. Respect and order are important, but a little silliness helps, too. Boys being boys, they sometimes walked backward and saluted backward. Sometimes, they made up intricate routines, substituting one boy for another until someone finally emerged to give the report. They danced. They wiggled. Sometimes an entire cabin stepped out together.

If the report was, "Not all present, and not all accounted for, Sir!" the questions started. "Who's missing? Where is he? Go find him." The reporting routine (and the chance to be first to get to the food) impressed on the campers their responsibility as individuals and as part of a group.

Raising and lowering the flag was an important part of Formation. Alex picked a cabin to do the honors and always rotated the choice between cabins. The cabin counselor then picked two campers, always mindful of giving everyone the same fair chance to be chosen. When Alex issued the order "Hands salute!" all hands saluted the flag as it was raised, with everyone keeping their eyes on the flag as it crept up the flagpole. "Crept" is the right word here. If you have ever stood at attention with your hand raised in salute as a six- or seven-year-old carefully pulls the rope, hand over hand, while the flag jerks up slowly, about three inches at a time, you know what I mean.

With the flag-raising in the morning came the Pledge of Allegiance followed by "Hands front!" and the hands came down. In the evening, the boys stood at attention as the flag was lowered and folded. This ceremony began and ended each day. It was predictable and gave the boys a chance to think ahead and decide if they wanted to volunteer for the responsibility of raising or lowering (and also properly folding) the flag.

Dave was only six years old when he first came to Flying Eagle with two older brothers. He spent the next twelve summers as a

camper, Kitchen Boy and counselor. He said his fondest memories were "hoping and hoping to be called on to ring the bell," "anticipating what activities we would be assigned during Formation," but also "dreading the responsibility of being asked to raise or lower the flag," with a special "ugh" for "folding it into a triangle."

Formation was a highlight in the memories of Bill:

Alex always expected us to look presentable for the ceremony, and with our shirts tucked in, hands and faces scrubbed. We'd take turns reporting on the present and absent members of the group. It taught us to not only be responsible for ourselves, but also for each other. We learned patriotism, discipline, cleanliness, responsibility, respect, community and camaraderie. The values he instilled in us will never go out of style.

Formation was an anchor in our structure. It gave us a chance to check on our campers throughout the day, to make announcements, present activities and congratulate campers on their accomplishments. The routine of flag-raising and lowering, the Pledge, and the history and spirit of Formation inspired orderliness and attention. Routine has a way of doing that.

The Bell

"The bell" was a huge part of our camp routine. It was a big, cast iron schoolhouse bell with a large, round clapper the size of a small cannonball. It stood at the side of the Chow Hall, next to the large cement patio. It had been given to us by the parents of one of our campers. Ringing the bell was an honor bestowed upon a camper who was already washed up and standing in front of the Chow Hall, ready to eat. Being picked to ring the bell became an incentive to get to the Chow Hall early.

A thick rope hung from the clapper and the boys had to pull or even push the clapper as hard as they could against its iron sides to make a loud enough ring. When they did, that bell could be heard all over the camp and all over the lake. Three slow rings were the signal that meant "line up at the Chow Hall." We rang the bell for every meal and to signal the start of special events.

One day the fire inspector was checking us out. "Do you have fire drills?" he asked. (Actually, we didn't.) "Do you have a way of getting all of the campers together if necessary?"

"Oh, yes," we said.

"Can you demonstrate?"

So we rang the bell. Not three slow rings. This time we kept it ringing. *Bong! Bong! Bong! Bong! Bong! Bong!* On and on. In less than a minute, campers and counselors came running in at top speed from *every* direction, skidding to a stop on the patio. Within two minutes, everyone was in front of the Chow Hall, lined up in cabin groups as at Formation, and wondering why. The inspector was astounded! We received a 100 percent rating!

Using the bell was our way of helping the boys become responsible for their own behavior. There was always a "first bell," and ten minutes later, a "second bell" before the start of any activity or meal. It was predictable, but non-judgmental, and it helped them learn how to plan their time and how to become responsible for themselves.

Do you have a consistent, non-judgmental way to give your young people an advance warning that a deadline is approaching? Music connected to a timer? Lights that flash on and off? A timer on their phone or watch? A reminder from Alexa? It is well worth the effort.

Mealtimes: Breakfast, Lunch and Dinner

It bears repeating—food is *hugely* important to active, growing boys. We could have easily spent half our time answering one question, "When are we going to eat?" Instead, the boys never had to ask because we ate at the same time every day. They sat together with their cabin group and counselor at assigned tables in the dining room. Meals were served family style in big bowls or on platters that were passed around the table. Each cabin was responsible for cleaning up after itself by scraping plates and throwing away paper products.

I learned about "growth spurts" at camp. It was amazing to see that when a boy hits age thirteen or fourteen, he starts to inhale food. Gallons and gallons of milk were downed at each meal by the boys in the older cabins. The KBs were always kept busy refilling bowls and platters with food.

First and Second Periods

Our Daily Program was an important part of reaching our goals, and a lot of thought went into scheduling each day's activities. It was more than making sure everyone had something to do. We wanted the boys to feel the pride that comes from trying something new and succeeding at it. Yet we also knew that if we let them pick their own activities, they might never try the ones they thought would be hard to do. So we scheduled activities by cabin. Because fairness was part of our philosophy, Dick always made sure that every cabin experienced each activity at least three times per session, with more time scheduled for favorite activities such as water skiing for the older boys or crafts for the younger ones. He scheduled two, hour-long activity periods in the morning and two in the afternoon—enough time to become engaged, but not bored.

We also made sure we allowed enough time between periods for campers to leave one activity and arrive on time for the next. We gave them ten minutes. They were responsible for getting to where they were supposed to be, but because our overall goal was to help them experience success, we made sure the schedule gave them enough time to run from one place to the next, take a bathroom break, stop off at their bunk to get something, or just visit with a friend and still make it to the next activity on time.

Not allowing enough time for transitions can set a lot of kids up for failure. When we allow enough time for them to get to where they need to be, whether at camp, at home or at school, we help them succeed and we save ourselves a lot of irritation and frustration.

Free Period!

Every day we gave the boys two, hour-long free periods. First and Second Period might have been scheduled by Dick, but Free Period was all theirs! At the breakfast and lunch Formation, Dick would announce three or four activities that would be open during Free Period. A camper could choose among them or he could choose to do something else such as lie on his bunk and listen to music, read a book, hang out with friends, or lie on the beach. Learning how to use "free time" constructively is a key component of future success. Many campers used the time to work on earning awards. Jon remembered "mad sprints to be first to waterski with hopes of getting in two runs in the same Free Period." The regular routine of Free Period gave campers a chance to anticipate and plan. The important point was that they were responsible for their own choices.

Rest Period!

Rest Period was the favorite period of the day for counselors! It came every day after lunch. Campers had to be on their bunks and quiet until 2:00 p.m. They didn't have to sleep, but they did have to be quiet. Mail from home was passed out during Rest Period. Campers read books, played cards, listened to music or wrote letters. It was a time of bliss for the staff.

From our perspective, Rest Period was also important because our minds need time to think and process information, unplugged from activity. Our laptops, tablets and smart phones can do a lot for us, but one thing they can't do is manifest the future from their computing. Only the human mind can do that, and that mind needs quiet downtime to think, reflect, visualize and plan. Had we kept campers busy every minute of the day in planned activities, it might have produced accomplishments and improved skills, but it would have taken away important opportunities for quiet reflection and the visualization of future success.

However, from a camper's point of view, Rest Period was probably most important for one reason—Candy Store! The Sugar Shack was open for Candy Store during Rest Period on Monday, Wednesday and Friday. Only two pieces of candy could be bought at one time and only if a camper brought a letter to mail home. As with everything else, access to Candy Store was governed by order and routine and fairness. Campers were called cabin by cabin and the order of going first was always rotated.

Anticipating something special like Candy Store, learning to wait for it and doing something responsible to "earn" it (such as writing a letter home), are all skills that serve us well as adults. In this case, we reinforced those skills three times a week with candy bars. A special treat doesn't have to be candy, but it ought to be something that isn't available every day.

Kool-Aid and Cookie Break!

Dinnertime wasn't until 6:00 p.m. and hungry boys are grumpy boys. Learning, teamwork and all-around good behavior are a lot easier to promote when kids aren't hungry. That's why the bell rang every afternoon at 3:00 and campers came running to the Chow Hall for Kool-Aid (otherwise known as "bug juice") and cookies. The Kool-Aid was cold and the cookies were big.

Evening Program

Because of daylight saving time, the summer sun does not set in our part of Michigan until 9:30 p.m., and twilight lasts for another half hour or so after that. Can you imagine trying to get a camp full of boys to go to sleep while it is still light out? It doesn't work. That is why, when Michigan began observing daylight saving time in 1972, Camp Flying Eagle didn't join in. We never moved the clocks forward and instead operated on "camp time." That meant the sun set in our world at 8:30 p.m. and all was dark by 9:00.

At 7:00 p.m., as the sun began to sink slowly behind the trees, it was time for Evening Program, an after-dinner, all-camp activity. A different activity was scheduled each night, and Dick would announce the choice at the dinner Formation. Everyone participated in some of them such as Council Fire and Skit Night, but others were optional, including games like baseball, ultimate Frisbee, Frisbee tag or the always-popular Capture the Flag. Any camper who wasn't tired after a full day of activities *had* to be after an hour of Capture the Flag. Participants were divided into two teams and the goal was to sneak behind the other team's line (a big chalk line down the middle of the baseball field) and capture their flag—a towel guarded by a goalie. The playing field involved all of the woods on either side of the field and a lot of running!

Some kind of physical, outdoor activity is a great investment in a good night's sleep. A walk around the block or even sit-ups together in the living room can help kids and adults sleep better. If fresh air and a lot of running aren't possible at the end of a day, sticking to a routine helps train young minds that the day is winding down and the time for rest is near.

Lights Out

A special part of our daily routine happened every night at Lights Out. Once the campers were in bed with the lights turned off, their counselor sat down on a bed or in a chair and by the light of a lantern or flashlight read aloud another chapter from an adventure book or mystery. From the youngest to the oldest, everyone settled down at night to listen to a story. "Bedtime story: I could hardly wait for the next night," Jim remembered.

Read to a child. Listening to the sound of your voice and of pages turning in the night, trying to focus on a story while drifting off to sleep, are wonderful ways for a child to end the day. The important point is to do it every night.

Our overall daily program was successful because routine is essential. Every Monday through Friday, the schedule was the same. There was a structure, rhythm and routine to the days and weeks of camp. The boys knew what to expect. Because of that, they could look ahead, think about and plan which awards they wanted to work on, how they would spend Free Period, and when they would write letters home so they could get those candy bars. Life was manageable and the boys were always in control because they felt the security of structure.

Following the Rules

Our structure did include rules. *Every* activity had safety rules. They were always in writing, always posted where they could be easily seen and were short and to the point:

> *Every person using the waterfront must sign in.*
>
> *Only one camper at a time. No double bouncing. (Trampoline)*
>
> *Shoes must be worn at all times, no flip-flops allowed. (Craft Shop)*

Keep in mind that once you set a rule, you will likely have violations. Because we knew that too many rules would lead to too many violations and that would have been counter-productive to the accomplishment of our vision, we focused on important ones.

Beyond the safety rules for activities and our emphasis on treating others and the camp wildlife with respect and kindness, we only had a few more. For example, except in an emergency, the bell could not be rung without permission, and anyone leaving or returning to the camp or an activity or campsite had to report in and out as we always had to know where everyone was at all times.

Other times, we minimized the need for rules by watching what the campers did naturally and incorporating it into our program. A little creative thought in the beginning can save a lot of headaches in the end. That's why during Rest Period the boys had to be on their beds, but didn't have to be lying down. And a camper didn't even have to be on his own bed, as long as he was on another camper's bed quietly playing cards or games.

It reminds me of a story about the construction of a new college campus with several buildings. Instead of pouring the sidewalks between the buildings right away, the architects waited to see where most students naturally walked. When they finally poured the concrete, they followed the paths already formed. That decision reduced the chance that students would cut across the grass, which, in turn, saved the grass, saved the grounds crew a lot of irritation and saved the students from breaking the rules.

The rules we did have were rigorously enforced, and there was a hierarchy of discipline when rules were broken. However, we also believed that most violations were the result of forgetfulness or over-excitement and we gave boys the benefit of the doubt. Counselors were not allowed to ban a boy from an activity, but they could give him a reminder or a warning, and if a boy violated an important safety rule, he might miss a turn at participation, giving him a chance to settle down. If the issue were more serious, it would be brought to the attention of Alex or Dick, who handled serious infractions by imposing the dreaded loss of Candy Store privileges or the running of a few laps around the baseball field, a great way to use up extra energy.

One camper, Gordon, whose memory still brings a smile, ran more laps than anyone else—*ever.* "How did that happen?" I asked Dick. "He was a good kid," he said, "but at night he was so excited that he was still laughing and talking and carrying on when everyone else was trying to sleep." I guess running laps did calm him down. He grew up to be a minister and keeps in touch with us.

Creative Consequences

Importantly, the consequence was not "punishment." There *is* a difference, just as there is a difference between "teaching" and "getting even." Effective teaching involves creative consequences for both appropriate and inappropriate behavior. A consequence for either should be linked to a privilege or something wanted, not something needed. The loss of Candy Store or having to spend time running or walking laps instead of going to a desired activity during Free Period were meaningful consequences in our camp world.

One way of developing a creative consequence is to explain the situation and why the desired behavior is important and then ask the child what he or she thinks is an appropriate response. We'd ask, "What's the best way to help you remember this?" If you think he is not likely to forget the whole conversation by the next day or to do "it" again before then and endanger himself, you might say you will think about it and let him know your decision later. You can be sure he will be wondering about it until "later" comes. There is nothing like allowing time for reflection to let a lesson sink in.

Can this be challenging? Yes. I once read a book that said our greatest teacher is the one we are living with. Of course, they meant husbands and wives and our capacity to drive each other crazy. When you live with another adult, it has the potential to bring to the surface all manner of irritations and disagreements that provide endless "opportunities" for personal growth. Some suggest that this is the essence of spiritual work, coming to realize that our conflict with others is rooted in our own perspective and that learning to love and accept others is the first step in learning how to love and accept ourselves. I think that's true, but it's not always easy.

Alex and I were married for over fifty years. When you put two strong-willed people together, there are bound to be many "opportunities" for personal growth. We did have our share, but as Alex would say, "we hung in there." He was very proud of that, and so am I. We kept trying to get "it" right by getting ourselves right.

Children give us that same chance. If our greatest teacher is the one we are living with, it applies to our children. They bring love and joy and happiness into our lives, but they also act as a mirror, reflecting back to us our hopes, our dreams, our fears, our embarrassment, our sense of responsibility and our pride. These little people have the ability to bring to the surface all of the hidden memories and beliefs that motivate us to act and react the way we do. You can be sure that whatever rules you set will be the catalyst. And when they are broken or violated, sometimes we get our response right, and sometimes we wish we had reacted differently.

Fortunately, every day presents a new opportunity for a "do-over." When my kids were young and outside playing whatever game was going on and someone's turn didn't go the way he or she thought it should, one had only to yell, *"Do-over!"* to claim the right to do it again and get a better result. Typically the others didn't say, "No, you can't! You failed, and now you are stuck with it!" No, the typical answer was a shrug and "ok." Where is it written you can't do it over? In fact, you can. If the future is created by our present, by the thoughts and emotions we now express, every day presents a new opportunity to reset the future machine in a new direction.

Of course, the difficulty often comes when you can't really identify what you need to change. All you really know is who you are, and the person you are makes sense to you. What you have learned throughout your life has taught you certain "truths," and you live your life by them. We all do. That would be fine if we lived by ourselves and didn't have to interact with others, but we do. Whether you have kids or teach kids or take care of kids, sooner or later you will face anger, frustration, fear and disappointment. These are all emotions that call on us to take action, to *do* something about it.

When that happens, when you feel those emotions, the best thing you can *do* is—pause. This is where the mission statement you have written out will help do for you what ours did for us at Camp Flying Eagle: help you refocus on the future and your ultimate goals. Review those goals and then give yourself some quiet time for reflection. This is why giving a child some time to wonder about what consequence he might be facing is such a good strategy—because it gives *you* time to think. Later, we've listed some resources that can help uncover hidden memories and beliefs that motivate us to act and react the way we do (and maybe in a way we'd like to change). Understanding those can help us narrow down our rules to the ones that matter the most and keep us from putting unnecessary roadblocks on a child's journey to success.

The more you know and understand yourself and your own underlying motivations, the better able you will be to focus on the rules that truly matter and to avoid the use of structure, routine and rules in a way that makes life harder for you and is counter-productive to the results you want to see. Our own camp journey taught us that rules are readily accepted when they aren't too onerous and there aren't too many, and if there is a good reason for them and they apply fairly to everyone. We learned that when discipline is fair, matter-of-fact and not angry, boys will rise to meet expectations, will conform their behavior and will focus their mental energy on achievement. When used as a part of a strategy for building future success, having structure, routine and rules will free a boy's energy to focus on future planning. And when his mental energy is focused on future success, it creates that success.

But, let's also acknowledge that, with boys being boys, even when you do everything right, there *will* be those times when you are really tested. And when that happens, it helps to have a sense of humor. It happened to us.

Tim was one of our very best counselors. He had been a camper with us for six years and had been awarded the coveted Camper of the Year award at our winter Camp Flying Eagle reunion. He then became a KB and a counselor. We trusted him completely. But one day, two of his campers turned up missing—the worst thing that can happen at a camp! Tim was frantic, and Alex was beside himself. Gordon and Bill were gone! The entire camp was searched. The waterfront was searched. The boats were counted. Nothing was missing.

Shortly thereafter, the missing boys sauntered back into the camp, fresh from their hike to the Blue Lake store, two miles down the road. Our counselors regularly hiked *with* boys to the Blue Lake store, where owners Kate and Curly (who was bald) always watched as the boys carefully examined the glass bottles of Nehi pop sitting in the cooler with their long necks sticking up through the ice water, showing different flavor-colored caps for the grape, orange and strawberry pop. But, going off by themselves broke every major rule we had.

"What is it you two boys are after?" Kate had asked.

They weren't after pop.

"Hydrogen peroxide."

Gordon and Bill ran *a lot* of laps that afternoon, yet somehow managed to hide the hydrogen peroxide from us. Fifty years later Bill told us, "We wanted to put it on our hair and turn it flaming red." And they did—on the very last day. At the end of the camp session, they greeted their parents with bright orange hair.

"What were we thinking?" he wondered. "Wait! We *weren't* thinking!"

And that's how it sometimes is with boys.

And when that happens, as it will, ask yourself whether it will really matter fifty years from now. And smile.

REMEMBER...

You are teaching your son who he is. Whether you do this consciously or subconsciously, you are training his mind to think a certain way about himself. We suggest you do it consciously. Through the use of structure and routine, your goal is to give him:

➤ A sense of belonging, confidence and mastery;

➤ A belief that he is a person who can learn what is expected and who believes that he is responsible for doing it;

➤ Opportunities to anticipate and plan;

➤ More mental energy to focus on learning;

➤ Opportunities to learn how to use "free time" constructively; and

➤ An environment where success is much more likely.

Your goal is to instill a sense of confidence and mastery through structure; to foster a feeling of being in control and competence because he "knows the routine" and can "work with it." You want him to come to believe that he is a person who can learn what is expected and can do it successfully. You are seeking to help give him opportunities to learn to anticipate and plan.

Keep in mind that when rules are used to control, instead of helping to create a foundation of future success, they take away self-mastery and can foster dependence and either timid or rebellious future behavior. Through the use of limited, but thoughtful rules, your goal is to teach, not punish, when violations occur.

CHAPTER SIX

— ACTION STEPS —

1. Think about how you might create a daily routine or schedule with an anchoring activity repeated every morning and every night.

2. How can you make it a practice to review the next day's activities with your son the day or night before? Highlight areas where he will have a choice to make about how to spend his time.

3. How can you build in a regular period of unstructured "free time"?

4. Make a list of all of the "rules" your son or students must follow. Rank them by importance.

5. For each rule, make a list of creative consequences for rule violations that do not include taking away a necessity (food, clothing, shelter, affection and caring). Your goal is to teach, not punish.

6. For recommended resources that deal with problem behavior, visit *www.TheFlyingEagleFormula.com/toolbox*

Dick, Tess and campers reading the day's newspapers on the patio in front of the Main Lodge

THE KEY TO SELF-ESTEEM

If you were to ask me today what I most wish for my children, I would say something like "happiness, fulfilling relationships with others, satisfaction with their lives, confidence and the knowledge that they can do whatever they set their minds to do." Success to me means being at peace with who you are, liking yourself and being confident enough to extend acceptance, joy, love and happiness to others.

Where does that confidence and that peace, love and joy come from? And why does it leave? When we look back on our own lives, has not our opinion of ourselves been shaped by the adults in them, especially when we were children? How many of us still struggle to overcome a belief that we are somehow not OK? Where did that come from?

An adult who believes in a child can unleash a powerful force of self-worth. Like a seed, it takes root; and once a seed of self-worth is planted, the tree will grow, with branches of confidence, satisfaction and success. Every day can present endless new opportunities to plant a seed of self-worth in a child.

While I was writing this, I received a call from Gloria, who wanted to tell me about a message she had just taken for Dick. It was from one of his former basketball players. "I am so sorry to have missed Coach," the caller said. "I wanted him to know that, next to my father, he was the most significant person in my life. He gave me a chance to do good and to be good. I will always love him for that. I'm a teacher now, trying to pass on all that he gave me." What a fine example of a lasting seed of self-worth well planted!

Dick still remembers what set off his own successful basketball, teaching and coaching careers. He was in the seventh grade and already a good basketball player. The high school coach came up to him, threw an arm around his shoulder and said, "You keep this up, kid, and you're going to be a whirlwind."

"I never forgot that word 'whirlwind,'" says Dick.

Beyond the words we say, another powerful way to plant seeds of self-worth is to show confidence in children by giving them opportunities to choose how to govern their own lives and to respect their choices, views and opinions—in other words, to validate the essence of who they are, what they think and what they feel.

Early in our camp adventure, we poured a large concrete patio in front of the Main Lodge and added a few chairs and a rustic coffee table. Every day, and especially on Sundays, the adult staff would sit out on the patio with a cup of coffee and read the paper. Boys were always welcome to stop by to sit and talk or read the paper with us, and they did. There on the patio, they would express their opinions about current events in the paper, especially baseball and other sports, and about camp happenings and events including their plans to earn a boatload of awards by the next Council Fire, and endless speculation on when Color War might be announced. We listened, we discussed, we respected their opinions and we got to *know* them.

I don't remember who suggested that we add the patio to the Main Lodge, but it was a great idea. In those interactions over nothing seemingly important was an important message: we respect your opinions, your views are important and we like talking with you.

Sharing important experiences with children, discussing them and valuing a child's input is another important way to show that you respect him and that his presence and opinion are important. Anyone can do this, at any time. If a special event were happening in the world outside of camp, we'd take our TV into the dorm and invite campers to watch and share it with us. Landing on the moon was one such event. Phil told us:

> *I was at camp when the US landed on the moon. I remember being able to stay up late to crowd around the TV and watch Armstrong take the first step, and I remember Alex telling us that we'll be tempted to get excited and cheer, but to be very quiet because Neil Armstrong will probably say something important. Alex was right, and Neil did, and if anyone asks me where I was when we landed on the moon, I'll know.*

Honoring Individual Choice About Personal Matters

Honoring a child's choice is another important way to sow seeds of self-worth. We found that a very effective way to convey respect was to provide daily opportunities for the boys to make choices about personal things and to honor those choices. When you let someone choose something for himself, you are telling him that he, as an individual, is responsible for himself and that you have faith in his judgment. That is why, even in our structured camp environment, we built in many opportunities for individual choice.

It started from the time the boys woke up in the morning. No one told them what to wear. They were in charge of picking out their clothes for the day, and the results were sometimes creative.

As adults, we worry about what other adults will think of us if our children show up creatively dressed. We worry that the kids won't "fit in." And sometimes the message we send is the opposite of what we intend. We want to say, "Let us help you look nice." Instead, we send this message: "You don't fit in. You aren't OK. Your decisions aren't good. Here's what you need." At Flying Eagle, beginning from the minute they woke up, the boys learned that we believed they were capable of making important personal decisions. (We did, however, eventually have to make a rule that they couldn't sleep in their swimsuits!)

Twice each day, they could choose how they wanted to spend Free Period. They could choose to go to one of the three or four areas scheduled to be open during Free Period, such as waterfront, archery, riflery or crafts, or to spend the time on something else, such as writing a letter, reading a book or visiting with friends. It was their choice. Having free time to make such choices is important for building self-esteem and initiative.

At lunch and dinner, no matter what else was being served, peanut butter and jelly and a loaf of bread were always out as an option for those who just didn't feel like eating what was on the menu. It was a way to treat campers as individuals, to give them a choice over something very personal and to say, "We respect your decision." What if a boy ate *only* PB&Js for *every* lunch and dinner? It didn't happen, but we do believe that most of us have an innate knowledge of what we need. We respected that. We made healthy choices available and let the boys choose among them. Bob said, "I was a camper from 1959–1962. My nickname was 'Pancake.' I held the camp record for eating twenty-two pancakes at one meal." Another accomplishment to celebrate!

Every Sunday morning, instead of a wake-up call at 7:20 a.m. followed by Formation and breakfast at 8:00, we served a drop-in smorgasbord breakfast from 8:00–9:15. We put out fruit, juice, cereal, doughnuts or coffee cake, meat and cheese, hard-boiled eggs, cocoa and milk. It was an easy breakfast to serve, but seemed special because of the choices it offered. Or, the boys could choose to skip breakfast altogether on Sunday and sleep in late.

Earning awards was all about personal choice. Our responsibility was to make the awards and opportunities available, but from there it was up to the boys. It was a personal decision and up to each boy to determine how many awards he earned and whether he swam the lake, took out boats, wrote stories for the camp newspaper, caught fish, got up early to jog or swim or bike, or took advantage of the many other opportunities.

We added choice to the routine in other ways. During the daily Rest Period campers could sleep, read, write letters and postcards, play cards or talk quietly, as long as they stayed on a bunk. Every Monday, Wednesday and Friday, as long as they had a letter to mail, they could choose between at least twenty different kinds of candy bars and candy at Candy Store: Slo-Pokes, Good & Plenty, Neccos, Root Beer Barrels, Atomic Fireballs, Pixie Stix, Three Musketeers, Mounds, Almond Joy, Twizzlers, M&M's... As Gloria or I stood there in the tiny Sugar Shack waiting...and waiting...and waiting... we *knew* the decisions were important because they took *so-o-o-o-o-o* long to make!

It wasn't that the choices were necessarily big ones, but they were about personal matters and that made them important. The every-day nature of the opportunity for choice also made a difference. It told the boys, "We are here, the fun is here, the opportunity is here, but it is up to you to choose how you will make your day." Every day that message was repeated and reinforced. The combination of that message and a daily message of "we respect you and we like you" is a powerful formula for planting seeds of self-worth and self-deter-mination that strengthen the foundation for a successful life.

Are there ways you can build personal choice into your son's everyday life? From picking out what he wants to wear, to choosing his own bath time, to deciding on his haircut? When an opportunity arises for your son to express his individuality, think long and hard about whether you really want to take that choice away.

REMEMBER...

Your goal is to give your boy daily messages that you believe in his competence and in his ability to be responsible for himself. You are embedding a belief in his mind that he *is* competent and able to take on responsibility.

CHAPTER SEVEN

ACTION STEPS

1. Make a list of all the ways you can build choice into your son's day.

2. Make it a practice to stop and listen to his opinions and thoughts about...whatever! Then use the three magic words: "Tell me more." Or these: "And then what?"

3. With personal computers and cell phones we often consume news online and by ourselves. Consider creating a weekly ritual of visiting a McDonald's or coffee shop or place where you can linger and talk. Take along a newspaper that you can split up and read. You are looking for "conversation starters." Read something interesting to each other and ask what he thinks about it.

Getting ready for a trip on the bus

CREATE A SOURCE OF STRENGTH

Structure and routine lead to traditions, and it is traditions that ground us. Tradition is something you and others "always" do or it is the way you "always" do it. Traditions create a sense of belonging, of being a part of something special and of something shared. Never underestimate the importance of the memory of belonging to something special.

Starting a tradition is easy. It doesn't have to cost money. Just look at what you "always" do, or will likely do again, and try to inject a little specialness, a little silliness or a little ceremony. A little bit of fun, a little bit of wonder and the desire to do it again make enriching traditions. A favorite song sung every time you leave on a trip or come back home, playing a favorite game only when it rains, watching a movie together every Sunday or camping out in the living room once a month are all easy ways to create the magic that helps create success.

Traditions by the week

There was a lot that was special about being at Camp Flying Eagle. It happened every day as part of the daily program, but also each week as part of the camp routine. One thing we learned from camper emails and letters is that memories of those traditions are long lasting. That's why somewhere, within at least half of all the letters and email we receive, are the initials PB&J and they don't mean the peanut butter and jelly that was available at lunch and dinner as an option for those who didn't want what was being served. They mean a Friday night tradition that still makes me cringe.

Every Friday night, before Council Fire was over, Gloria and I went to the kitchen where we were sometimes joined by the KBs. There we would all scoop up Jif peanut butter with big, rubber spatulas and spread it on slice after slice of white bread. We'd spread grape and strawberry jelly on more white bread until we'd made about eighty PB&J sandwiches, enough for the whole camp.

After Council Fire, when the boys were in bed with their teeth already brushed and their faces clean, Alex and Dick would come around with big trays of PB&J sandwiches to be eaten as they lay in their beds under the covers. Crunchy? Creamy? We took special orders. Don't like peanut butter? No problem. You can order plain jelly. You only like grape jelly? No problem. Don't like jelly? No problem! You can special order a sandwich with just peanut butter. How did that ever start? Who thought of such a thing? It must have been Alex. But the boys loved it! It became a favorite memory. I think they still have all of their teeth. At least I hope they do!

Counting echoes at Council Fire evolved into another tradition. Behind the Council Fire, the woods led down to a valley with a marsh at the bottom and another hill in the distance beyond. Somehow it was perfect for creating echoes. At the start of every Council Fire, Alex would lead the campers in a special yell. Like a conductor, he would get the whole camp to yell in unison and then cut the yell off sharply so that everyone could listen for the echoes and count them.

The close of Council Fire evolved into yet another tradition. With arms crossed right over left, the campers and counselors held hands in a human chain and quietly sang and then hummed taps:

Day is done, gone the sun.
From the lakes, from the hills, from the sky.
All is well, safely rest.
God is nigh.

The campers then walked single file in silence back down the Council Fire path. It was a thoughtful time and a solemn ending to the day. I'd like to believe they were lost in the beauty and meaning of the setting, but I don't think so. The very second a camper's foot left the Council Fire path and touched the outermost edge of center field, it was a free-for-all. They ran at full speed, whooping, hooting and hollering as loud as possible, all the way back to their dorm or tent. I don't know how that tradition first started, but it was probably the anticipation of the PB&Js to come.

Another favorite camp tradition was bingo. It was special because we only played bingo when it rained. A rainy day can be a disaster for a camp, but not at Flying Eagle. I always kept a stash of candy bars, flashlights, baseball caps, Frisbees and other goodies to use as prizes. We wrapped them in the Sunday funnies and played until we ran out.

In August, when meteor showers and falling stars are common, we started another tradition. Without streetlights to dilute the darkness, we can see millions of stars. The Milky Way is clear and awe-inspiring, and we sometimes saw spectacular displays of the Northern Lights. A favorite pastime was spotting and counting the tiny moving satellites that circle the Earth. Campers and counselors brought sleeping bags out to the middle of the baseball field to lie under the stars and watch the display.

Traditions by the trip

One way to create a tradition is to take a trip to the same place every year. One of our most anticipated traditions came twice each summer when we took an all-camp trip each session to Mackinac Island. Mackinac Island is a historic island and resort in Lake Huron between Michigan's Upper and Lower peninsulas. Fort Mackinac was established there by the British during the Revolutionary War, and the fort still stands today as a tourist attraction. The entire island is a national historic landmark and is filled with quaint shops and hotels, including the famous Grand Hotel, which boasts the world's longest front porch and was the setting for the movie *Somewhere in Time*. No cars are allowed on the island, and horses and buggies are everywhere. In 2014, it was voted one of the United States' Top 10 Best Islands and in 2018 was named the #1 Summer Destination by Trip Advisor.

It usually took us two hours to reach the island from the camp, one hour by bus and another by boat. Picture a bus filled with young boys, ages seven to thirteen, singing "Ninety-nine Bottles of Beer on the Wall" *all the way* down the highway. Multiply that by *the entire day* and you'll have some idea of what it was like.

There comes a point in the trip along I-75 where, if you know where to look, you can see the majestic spans of the Mackinac Bridge rising over the tops of the trees. The bridge is the world's third longest suspension bridge and it connects the two Michigan peninsulas. The first camper to spot the bridge won a candy bar. It was another tradition that kept the bus trip exciting—and interrupted the bottle countdown.

The bus trip was only part of the adventure. After parking in Mackinaw City, we'd head for the ferryboat that would take us to the island. Even after speedier catamarans began shuttling passengers to the island in under half an hour, we always took the slower, more leisurely ferry. To be on a double-decker ferryboat, plowing through the waters of Lake Huron, with the sun beating down as seagulls circle overhead looking for popcorn, is a memorable experience.

After we docked, the first order of business was always a picnic on the hillside in front of Fort Mackinac. Never forget: food first. Then a chance for each boy to decide how he'd spend his time: a tour of the fort or a bike ride around the island.

As wonderful as those choices were, it was the last half hour on the island that the campers loved most. That's when they were each given five dollars to spend at the small shops that line the main street and sell a huge variety of tourist souvenirs. The boys loved the shopping, but boys being boys, there were always some who came back with souvenirs that we had to confiscate and hold until the end of the camp session—like bullwhips, jack knives, rubber girly dolls that could be squeezed until their breasts popped out, nudie playing cards or other items. We looked stern and gave them lectures, but we were never mad. An eight-year-old with nudie cards? Really? It was just too funny.

Even the return trip was memorable because traveling back to the camp included an uphill climb on the highway in an old bus filled with campers and counselors. When the bus would start to slow down, Dick, an extraordinary bus driver, would shift to a lower gear. You could hear the bus strain as it went even slower up the hill. Dick would shift again and soon every camper, from the tall to the small, would be chanting: *"Go Bus, Go! Go Bus, Go!"*

They also leaned forward, as if that would help. Usually it worked, but sometimes it didn't and we'd all have to pile out of the bus and walk up the hill with the empty bus chugging along beside us. No one minded. It made the adventure even more memorable. Our last stop was always a camp ground and a cookout. When it comes to boys, food makes everything better.

Another great tradition was the trip we took each summer to the Sleeping Bear Dunes. Overlooking Lake Michigan, these sand dunes are preserved as a national lakeshore park. Bluffs tower 450 feet high. Every year a few of our campers and counselors would hike up the bluffs, across the dunes and make their way to Lake Michigan on the other side. But most campers spent the day climbing up the seemingly endless mountain of shifting sand, again and again in the hot sun, and rolling or jumping or running or tumbling all the way back down, emerging with sand in their hair, sand in their pockets, sand in their pants—sand everywhere. They loved it!

Traditions in song

Any song can become a tradition. "Ninety-nine Bottles of Beer on the Wall" was only one of many camp songs that were not only camp traditions, but *powerful signs of belonging.* Two of the others were "Ki Yi Ki Yike Us" and "KillyKillyKilly." The campers loved to sing them:

> *Ki Yi Ki Yike Us!*
> *Nobody likes us!*
> *We are the boys from Crooked Lake!*
> *Always a winnin'*
> *Always a grinnin'*
> *Always a feelin' GREAT!*

Nobody likes us? I tried suggesting that the words were probably supposed to be "Nobody's like us," but no one agreed, and they happily sang it the other way every year.

The other one was even stranger:

> *Killy, killy, killy, killy,*
> *Watch, watch, watch, watch,*
> *Kay you killy com kow wah!*
> *Killy, killy, killy, killy,*
> *Watch, watch, watch, watch,*

Kay you killy com kow wah!
Hail Camp Flying Eagle! Flying Eagle polly wah!
Hail Camp Flying Eagle! Flying Eagle polly wah!

What does that even mean? Whatever the songs meant, if you knew them it was a sign you belonged. Phil, a camper from 1967–1969, told this story:

> *I went to the University of Michigan in the early '80s. After a year of college, I took about five years off before returning to school, so I was an older student (at least relative to the other underclassmen). In one of my classes, we got to talking about things we had done in our lives. Specifically, our professor was urging us to remember songs and lyrics we had learned throughout our lives.*
>
> *I was surprised when one guy started singing the Flying Eagle song, and we got to talking. He had gone to camp a good 10 years after I had. It was an odd kind of linkage but it reminded me of how that place didn't just help some kids grow up. Its influence truly spanned generations.*

"Special Night" Traditions

Because every Thursday night was the cook's night off, Cookout Night became a Thursday night tradition with campers making plans with their counselor to conquer a new location each week for their outdoor meal. Older campers would hike down the road to Sand Lake, a hidden gem in the forest. For younger campers, the favored spot was "Forty Pines," about two miles away. This was a stand of white pine that had somehow evaded the lumberjacks' saws at the turn of the century with trees now majestically tall. A cookout with a campout at Forty Pines would earn the young campers three awards: Hiking, Campfire, and Overnight. Even now, we hear of former campers returning once again to sleep under the Forty Pines.

Watching a movie together on a regular basis is an easy tradition to start. Movie Night was a Saturday night tradition that required a letter home for admission. Campers came to Movie Night in their pajamas with pillows and blankets to stretch out on the floor. At first, we rented movies that came on 16 mm film. Alex would pore over a large catalog of available films and select the movies. He really enjoyed that. Every week, the movies would arrive in the mail. They came on large, circular reels about sixteen inches in diameter with two or three for each movie. The reels arrived in the mail in a large, square metal box with green canvas straps holding it together. That was the 1950s and '60s version of Netflix.

I can still see Alex mounting a full reel of film onto the projector and then pulling out a foot or two to feed into a slot on the projector's empty reel where it would catch and pull tight, ready for the movie to unwind from the first reel to the second as it passed through the bright light of the projector's lamp. I can still hear the whirring of the reel and the slightly scratchy sound as the movies and the music jumped to life. Rich, a camper from 1971-1975 told us, "I still remember *Bridge on the River Kwai* and *Guns of Navarone* like they were yesterday." The 1958 black and white movie *The Fly* also became a camp classic, with the guy trapped in a fly's body crying, "Help me...!"

Sharing "the point of it all"

Church is an ongoing tradition for many families that we continued at camp. Boys who got up early for church were always the first in the Chow Hall on Sunday morning. Catholic campers went to Mass with Dick and Gloria. We took other campers to various places of worship if requested by their parents. For everyone else we offered a Sunday morning tradition called Green Chapel, a non-denominational discussion at the Council Fire. The stillness, the quiet and the beauty of the trees along with Alex or Dick's unique talks held the boys' attention.

Those talks would be a discussion or story about desirable characteristics and qualities of a good person: integrity, industriousness, courage, helping others and being fair and trustworthy. Whatever the topic, Alex would frequently use his own experiences to emphasize his point or he would discuss stories with a lesson from Aesop or other writers. When an adult takes time to share stories of personal experience, it makes an impact. Dave told us how much Green Chapel meant to him:

> *My most significant memories, my most impactful memories of my adult life, are the memories I have of Green Chapel. Every Sunday morning, we would quietly walk across the ball field to that sacred place in the trees where Council Fire was held. There, Alex, and occasionally Coach Black, would bestow upon us the wisdom of their experiences and beliefs.*
>
> *Never was there a denominational component, never were we told what to believe. But when we were asked to close our eyes and just listen, listen to the leaves rustling, listen to your neighbor breathing, listen to the bee buzzing, you just KNEW, there was something bigger than you out there.*

The importance of the tradition of Green Chapel lay in its message. In the process of growing up, we all face situations that leave us questioning "the point of it all." An important part of a successful life is the ability to go on in the face of crisis and doubt. Having an answer to "What's the point of it all?" can make the difference. When that answer is steeped in tradition, it is lodged in our memory where it can rise up to help us when we need it.

Going to church is, of course, a wonderful way to regularly share perspective, especially if you add to it a tradition of personally discussing your beliefs. Today, however, not all families have the opportunity to gather together for church or haven't yet found a spiritual home. No matter. Whether you belong to a particular religion or none at all doesn't matter. What does matter is that you share with the children you love your understanding of "the point of it all" and that you do it regularly and make it enjoyable.

Together you can watch Joel Osteen or another inspirational speaker on TV, or episodes of The Andy Griffith Show, widely praised for its gentle teaching of positive values. Read a chapter each week from a book by an inspirational author. Volunteer to serve food at a homeless shelter. Collect clothes for those in need. Hold your own Green Chapel and share a different story from your own life each week, one where you learned an important lesson. Share yourself.

Most important, share your feelings. As adults, we sometimes try to forget how we feel. Instead, we discuss and lecture. But children and young people *feel* very strongly. Share with them how *you* would feel, as in, "It would *break my heart* if you used drugs." It was former IBM executive Bill Oliver, who fought to keep his own daughter off drugs and alcohol and started the national drug prevention initiative Parent-to-Parent, who noted that you can't assume that children will "pick up" your beliefs or feelings just from being around you. "I made the assumption," he said, "that because my children watched what we did, they knew what we think. It's not true. Today you have to verbalize your beliefs."

Remember, in today's world where all manner of thoughts and beliefs are shared online and made available to our children, what *you* actively share with them is more important than ever. The point is to create a tradition of sharing yourself, your thoughts, your feelings, your beliefs and your perspective.

This is especially important for children and teens who don't yet have the perspective that comes with our later years that shows us that somehow, someway, things tend to work out—that somehow, we do get through difficult times. Nick Vujicic, who was born without arms or legs, tells how he almost drowned himself at the age of 10 because he was in despair believing that he would never get married, never be able to hold his wife's hand and never hold a job. But despite his very real daily difficulties and the bullying he endured, his parents had deeply shared themselves, and he knew they loved him. It was the thought of their absolute sorrow that stopped him from committing suicide. Today he has a different perspective. Now, still with neither arms nor legs, he is married with four beautiful children and is successfully sharing a message of hope with the world.

Share yourself. Share important lessons. Share your understanding of "the point of it all." The little time you take now to share will help keep your children on a path of success.

On the other hand, I know that there was at least one Green Chapel lesson that wasn't as effective as it was meant to be. Debbie told me that one year a counselor shared a story about a carpenter who was known far and wide for his excellent work and fair prices. The carpenter never made much money, but he took great pride in his work. One year, he said to himself, *everyone else is cutting corners and making much more money. I should, too.* The very next day, when a man asked him to build a house, the carpenter agreed, but this time, wherever he could, he cut corners. It bothered him, but he told himself that the homeowner would never know. As a result, he was able to make a much larger profit and was quite satisfied with himself. When the home was finished, the man came to the carpenter. "You have always done such excellent work and so unselfishly," he said as he held out the keys. "This house is for you."

"As a child," Debbie said, "when I heard him talk about "cutting corners,"" I pictured something that looked like the sides of a stop sign. For years, I just assumed that it was somehow cheaper to make houses with the corners chopped off. But I did wonder how the homeowner wouldn't see that the corners weren't square. It was a long time before I realized that 'cutting corners' meant taking short cuts or not doing things in the best possible way."

A Tradition of Special One-Time Events

If Sunday morning was reserved for Green Chapel, Sunday afternoon was reserved for special all-camp events such as Water Carnival, which featured water races like a canoe race without paddles. The boys could only paddle with their hands and had to jump in and out of the canoe every time a whistle blew. As the canoes filled up with water, the boys had to keep paddling as they tried to race the completely submerged canoes. Other favorite competitions included a relay race through knee-deep water carrying a hard-boiled egg back and forth on a spoon and "water polo" between two teams played with a greased watermelon. A greased watermelon forced under water and then let go will shoot to the surface like a rocket!

Field Day was another Sunday afternoon event and always included an egg toss with raw eggs. There is a special technique to catching a raw egg being tossed at you from twenty, thirty, even forty feet away. I'm not sure I ever mastered it. Fortunately, I was usually paired up with a six- or seven-year-old and they can't throw very hard or very far!

Another fun tradition was Camper-Counselor hunt. We held this once per session during Evening Program. It gave the campers a chance to match wits with the counselors. When the bell rang, the campers would have twenty minutes to disappear into the forest. Out beyond the baseball field, the heavy ferns could easily hide a small, very quiet, very still camper. Some hid in the stumps of large trees. Others covered themselves with branches. When the bell rang again, the counselors had only twenty minutes to find the campers. Any camper who hadn't been found when the bell rang for the third time would win...what else? A candy bar! That's why, as the counselors moved through the woods, you could hear them yelling:

"Candy bars! Come out little candy bars!"

Bob told us:

> *I never saw ferns before, and maybe just a few birch trees. I remember lying under the ferns during the camper-coun-selor hunt, hoping not to be found, but afraid I'd be stepped on. Wondering if time was up yet. Hearing counselors yelling 'candy bars!' Did that mean the hunt was over and I had won? I didn't move. My counselor walked right past me, but "didn't see me" (right!) I won a candy bar!*

Knowing that the next year would bring another chance to triumph over the counselors, campers made elaborate plans for how and where to hide the next time. Matt remembers one year trying to hide in a tree. "But I was spotted!" he says. "The next year, I prepared a spot with lots of leaves and branches and eluded detection!" Success!

Skit Night was a favorite Evening Program tradition that also only came once each session. Each cabin was responsible for putting on a skit, and they were as bad and as corny and as juvenile as you can imagine. I don't know what it is about young boys' sense of humor, but it always seemed to involve bras and wigs, cream pies and a lot of pretend peeing with water on any unsuspecting counselors and camp directors they managed to trick into "helping" with the skit. "Please?! Please?! Please?!" they would insist. "We just need you to sit *right here*...."

Traditions are hard to break because of this...

Once they start, traditions can be hard to break, whether you like them or not. The key to changing them is to recognize the import-ant role they play in creating a sense of continuity, of belonging and of being part of something with history. These are all powerful desires that we meet with traditions, and if you want to change one, you need to replace it with another.

One tradition I never liked very much came on August 11th, Alex's birthday. It started one year when the counselors ambushed him at Formation. They carried him, kicking and squirming, down the hill to the lake with the campers following and shouting "DOWN TO THE LAKE! DOWN TO THE LAKE!" They managed to get him out onto the dock, and then with the count of 1, 2, 3, they heaved him into the lake fully clothed. The campers loved it, and then they jumped in, too—also fully clothed. Thereafter it became an annual event.

I never liked it because I was always afraid that they might drop Alex as they carried him down the cement steps to the lake. We all agreed that he needed to end it, but how? Finally, he told the campers, "Enough is enough," and negotiated a grand bargain to replace an old tradition with a new one. The price? Banana splits. The campers cheered, and a new tradition began.

The shared experiences and traditions, the familiarity of the daily program and the weekly routines gave our campers that sense of belonging, grounding and security that reproduces itself in the future. The experience of secure relationships leads a child to envision and *expect* a future of belonging and security like the past he remembers and knows.

Ideas Leave Not Their Source

Is there a downside to tradition and belonging? Well, sure. When tradition and belonging go beyond fostering a warm feeling of security and instead become like a straightjacket that suffocates individuality and creativity, they cease to be a means of manifesting success and instead become about power and control.

I've heard it said that "ideas leave not their source." What does that mean? It means that if we create the future by the thoughts we think now and the vision we have of that future, then the very reason we decide to do something also influences the future. It's like a flavoring we give to a cake we are baking. If you put in chocolate flavoring, you're not going to get a vanilla cake. "Ideas leave not their source" means that the reason you decide to do something will impact its ultimate outcome. The very same activity, undertaken with a different purpose in mind, will produce different results. Think carefully. What flavoring do you want to add to the future?

What does this have to do with tradition and belonging? Just this. If your primary purpose is to impose order because you expect problems and you want to make your own life easier, you can be sure that you will get problems and a lot of unhappy fallout on the kids around you. If, however, you have carefully crafted a vision with the goal of giving kids the kind of experiences that foster security and belonging, you will get a different result altogether.

It's also true that any one of these "ingredients," focused on while others are excluded, will produce an unbalanced result. Tradition and belonging have to be balanced with respect and choice. Structure, routine and rules have to be balanced with fun. When we keep in mind our vision for the future and *why* we want to foster traditions and a sense of belonging, we set in motion the results we seek.

Reflect for a moment on your own life and ask yourself whether and how the presence or absence of a deep feeling of belonging and security has shaped your life, your relationships and your ability to reach your full potential. Help the children around you create a future of success by creating an experience of tradition and a deep feeling of belonging and security now.

REMEMBER...

Your goal is to create a deep feeling and belief of belonging and security through traditions.

CHAPTER EIGHT

—— ACTION STEPS ——

1. What are some activities you "always" do or will likely do again? What specialness (a stop for ice cream?), silliness (a song you sing on the way?), or ceremony (a special prayer or saying?) can you add to it?

2. What tradition can you start in order to share your personal view of "the point of it all" with stories or examples from your life?

3. Consider creating your own family "Green Chapel" either every week or once a month.

CFE made such an indelible impression on me that I took a 'side trip' coming from Up North with my 12- and 9-year-old daughters and visited the camp. It was a beautiful, sunny day like they always used to be. As I stepped out of my car, the memories came flooding back. We walked the playing field and the path to the bonfire site. Walked past the younger kids' cabin (where I was Color War captain the year we won it and got 'all the ice cream you could eat').

The memories are too great to count, but a few of them are: bug juice, last finger to the nose had to 'scrape' the plates, softball, pinball bombardment on the basketball court, movie night, Candy Store, bear scares, rolling up the tent flaps and listening to the wind rustling the leaves, after lunch quiet time, letters from home, thunderstorms in the tent, going to Dead Man's Hill on a long bike trip, 40 Pines, canoeing the Manistee, Daddy Long Legs everywhere, getting the new CFE tee shirt every year. CFE was a core part of a very happy childhood."

Rich (camper, 1971–1975)

A "Big Wheel" used by Michigan loggers in the 1800s

RAISE A CREATIVE PROBLEM-SOLVER

O ne thing we can be sure of: the successful among us have learned the art of creative problem solving. Where did they learn that? And can it be learned? Yes, it can, and in a fun, enjoyable and easy way.

The ability to solve problems creatively depends on a mind that is free to consider alternatives, to think of options and to "think outside the box." A great way to open the mind to such options is by learning more about the world around you. Not only does that lead to greater wisdom, greater confidence, a sense of place and of being grounded, but more important, new experiences keep the mind open to receiving new ideas. In fact, we now know that when the mind encounters and processes new information, it expands. New neural connections form as new information is absorbed. This is an especially powerful process in our youngest years. Childhood presents us with a window of opportunity to grow the brain's capacity to be open to and process new information. It is that openness that will enable our children to seize new opportunities for success when they later appear.

By deliberately encountering new and different experiences and opinions, we send a message to our subconscious mind that it is ok to be open to new information. The human brain has the ability to take in and store huge, vast amounts of information. If we were aware of all of it, all of the time, we would have difficulty focusing. Instead, every day we tell our own minds what to pay attention to and what to ignore. Our mind then brings to our attention more of what we've said to pay attention to, and ignores the rest. But creative problem solving calls for an ability to consider what we might have been ignoring.

A lot of folks like to repeat the quote that, "the definition of insanity is doing the same thing over and over again, but expecting different results." What's missing is that you then have to be able to think of something different to do, to try. Unless we have given our mind permission to consider new and different information, it will be difficult to come up with a different way of doing things. You want to build that ability into your son from a young age. We did that by introducing our campers to new and different experiences. Our philosophy said: "We believe young people need opportunities to explore the world around them." It was up to us to create those opportunities.

Create An Open Mind By Exploring Local Places

Every place offers unique features to explore, and so it was with Crooked Lake. The discovery of the rusty fry pan was just the beginning. Other campers soon found old, rusty railroad spikes that were used to secure iron railroad tracks to wooden railroad ties. It turned out that an old railroad ran right across our baseball field. One of our neighbors, who settled the lake in the 1930s, told us that a railroad junction had been only a mile away where coal and sawdust piles were still visible, along with apple trees planted by the lumbermen who stayed in little cabins with their families. The former railroad beds were built by Swedish immigrants and were elevated with ditches on either side called 'Swede holes.' He also told us about Deward, a ghost town four miles away on the Manistee River.

Railroad beds? Swede holes? A ghost town? It didn't take long for the news to spread through the camp. We learned that Deward was built when the lumber baron who owned the land died in 1900 and his will instructed that all of his land be lumbered within twelve years. In those twelve years, Deward grew to include forty homes, a boarding house, a church, a school, a baseball team and a company doctor. But when the lumber was gone, Deward died.

Our older campers headed to Deward with a metal detector to see what they could find. They were rewarded with a huge, rusty circular saw blade, which they somehow managed to bring back. It was nailed to the museum wall. Soon, all the cabins wanted to go exploring. They became very good at tracking the long-ago railroad beds and finding all kinds of treasures: spikes, bolts, old bottles, an engine's steering wheel, a railroad coupler and pin, a lantern and jugs. We added their treasures to the museum, to brag about, to learn about and for all to see.

With so many artifacts, we all wanted to know more about the history that surrounds us. Only twenty miles away is Hartwick Pines State Park with its large stand of majestic, old-growth white pines that survived the lumberjacks. Some of the trees date back to the 1600s and are now huge and up to fifteen stories high.

Michigan was once covered with those huge white pines, hundreds of years old, but under the 1856 and 1857 land grant laws passed by Congress, companies that built railroads in Michigan, Wisconsin and Minnesota were given the land around the railroad by the federal government. That meant that a railroad line built from southern to northern Michigan didn't necessarily need passengers and freight to make money as long as the line traveled through well-forested areas because the lumber could be cut and sold. And that's what happened. In the late 1800s and early 1900s, loggers moved in and cut down nearly every tree. Even today, their massive stumps, five, six, even seven feet across, dot the landscape.

The trees filled the boys with wonder and awe, and the Hartwick Pines logging museum taught them about the life of the lumber-jacks in the 1800s. Seeing bunk beds stacked three beds high and the Big Wheel carts used to haul lumber out of the forest always made the trip memorable. We found copies of old photographs of the lumbermen and logging operations that we framed and added to our museum wall.

Every place I've ever lived has had unique features and opportu-nities to learn, explore and expand horizons. When I was growing up in Canajoharie, New York, you could tour the local Beech-Nut Packing Company factory, watch them make gum and candy and, the best part, get samples as you left. In Lansing, Michigan, where we lived in the winter, we visited the zoo, watched Oldsmobiles being manufactured at the General Motors plant and saw magnif-icent views of stars and planets at the Michigan State University planetarium.

Because of my own experiences, I was constantly looking for new things in the area to explore with the boys. We didn't have to look far. The stones that sparkled along the side of the road after a rain turned out to be Petoskey stones. Nowhere else in the world are they found as abundantly as they are in Northern Michigan. Petoskey stones are fossilized colonies of coral, formed some 350 million years ago when Michigan was under seawater. The tiny sea coral grew a six-sided shell to live in. As it grew, it produced buds, which made their own six-sided shells. Each year the coral grew taller and wider, spreading like a bouquet of flowers. When you find a Petoskey stone you have really found a coral colony, and often an entire colony preserved in stone. Their great popularity, in addition to their uniqueness and beauty, comes from the fact that they are soft enough to be sanded into shapes. Michigan tourists can take home beautiful Petoskey stone jewelry in the form of pendants, earrings, cuff links and rings.

For the boys, rainy days could mean a hike to search for the stones, and a chance to stomp all of the water out of every puddle they found and onto fellow campers! We'd bring the Petoskeys back to our craft shop and polish them with fine-grade sandpaper. Later, we bought tumblers to help polish the rocks. These are canisters you fill with rocks, abrasive powder and water. As the canister turns and the rocks tumble, the powder polishes them. Our first one ran on wind power, but it seemed to take forever to polish the stones. "The boys will be back home before we ever see one shiny rock," I complained to Gloria. So we bought an electric tumbler that did a much better job, and the boys could proudly show off their shiny rock treasures when they left.

With all of the interest in rocks, especially among the younger boys, I'd often drive a group of them over to a nearby small rock quarry where the boys learned to identify a variety of rocks and fossils and build collections for their science award. It also gave them something to show off back home.

Deadman's Hill was another local destination we explored. It is an area about forty-five minutes from the camp that overlooks a very steep drop-off into the Jordan River Valley. It's named as a memorial to Big Sam, a twenty-three-year-old lumberjack from the early 1900s. The story goes that in 1910, on the day Big Sam was to marry his childhood sweetheart, he was driving a team of horses down the hillside with a Big Wheel loaded with timber. The cart slipped and ran over him, killing him instantly. In the autumn, when the leaves of the sugar maples turn a brilliant red, and those of the quaking aspens turn yellow, the view over the valley of hills and gullies can be breathtaking. It is a fitting tribute to Big Sam.

The campers didn't care about the view. For them, the attraction was the challenge of the hill. A sandy trail leads down the hillside at a steep angle. At the bottom is the Jordan River, sometimes a trickle, sometimes more. It was a challenge getting down, but the real challenge was climbing back up. We didn't have an award for that, but we could have!

Exploring Distant Places

To further expand the boys' horizons, we added cabin trips, the kind of trips the boys weren't likely to have made before, such as long-distance bike trips, overnight canoe trips down the Manistee River and three-day camping trips into the wilderness of Michigan's Upper Peninsula, the "U.P.," with its beautiful Pictured Rocks National Park.

The impact of such new experiences can last a lifetime. Phil told us:

> *Throughout my life, I have always had an interest and desire to go off the beaten path and explore the obscure and unusual. I have usually traced the origins of this pastime back to Camp Flying Eagle, when we would go off and cruise around the U.P., looking for adventures great and small. That was my favorite part of the camp, and it is the part of Flying Eagle that has stayed with me for all the days of my life.*

With each successful trip, the boys learned more about the world around them and bonded with cabin mates. They gained knowledge, a sense of accomplishment and the confidence that goes along with it. Bill, a counselor for the U.P. trips, remembers:

> *The bus trips into the UP with campers still remain one of my fondest memories. I have been north several times with my family and always tried to retrace our bus route through the southern shore of Lake Superior, remembering*

the swims at the Lower Tahquamenon Falls, hikes back to the Upper Falls and side trips to Paradise and Whitefish Point. I never spent a night again like we did in those days when we just threw our sleeping bags on the sand and slept under the stars.

Of course, no matter the age, trips with boys are always…interesting. The Mohawks were the second youngest cabin and typically eight years old. This is the story they wrote about their canoe trip down the Manistee River:

We saw an otter and one deer. One of the canoes tipped over and Terry lost one of his shoes and one sock. Scott lost one of his shoes, too. We saw 20 girls. They started when we started. They stopped to get their bathing suits on. We took pictures of them. At the CCC Bridge, we threw sand and we splashed them. Then our counselor said we couldn't have our dessert.

Exploring Different Cultures

Expanding horizons doesn't always have to be about visiting new and interesting places. Living in a tent or small dorm room with six or seven other boys you don't know, from different parts of the state, country, and even other countries, is eye-opening and world expanding. At the same time, when you have friends from so many different places, both the country and the world seem smaller, more familiar and more manageable.

But leave it to boys to put their own spin on it. One year, an airline pilot, whose route included Mexico, sent his sons to Flying Eagle. He was so delighted with their growth and development that he spread the word to people he knew well. Soon boys from Mexico joined us. It was a great opportunity for boys from neighboring countries to get to know one another, live together and appreciate differences on matters of importance to young boys such as the

Americans' skill at baseball and the Mexicans' skill at soccer. But, we soon found out that nine, ten, and eleven-year-old boys are mostly the same everywhere. It's possible that our lasting contribution to world understanding is that they learned swear words in two languages!

REMEMBER...

Your goal is to send a message to your son's subconscious mind that it is ok to think about, learn about, and consider new information.

CHAPTER NINE
ACTION STEPS

1. Consider finding older people in your community who are willing to share their life stories as a way to "explore" without going far.

2. Is there a family from another country you can invite to dinner?

3. Can you visit a nearby exhibit or tour a nearby factory that showcases how things are made or done? When you keep in mind the vision of the outcome you are seeking, finding new places to explore becomes more than just "something to do." It becomes a cornerstone of a success mindset.

Kool-Aid and Cookie Break!

THE BEST WAY TO IMPROVE RESULTS

I s fun part of success? Ask fans of the Chicago Cubs. The Cubs, shut out of championships for over 100 years, started to change with the hiring of new manager Joe Maddon in 2014. He came to work each day with a light-hearted approach. Late in 2015, he invited a flamingo, a penguin, a sloth and a baby snow leopard into the clubhouse to hang out with the team, and that year they won a playoff spot for the National League Championship, their first playoff appearance since 2003. In 2016, the team wore T-shirts emblazoned with some advice Maddon gave to a newly arrived player, "Try not to suck." It became their unofficial slogan, and in 2016, they won the National League Championship *and* the World Series.

What Makes Something Fun?

If our goal is to help kids experience success, a good dose of fun can help. Whether you are at home, in a classroom or on the job, adding fun into the mix will improve results. What makes something fun? Sometimes it's hard to remember just how much fun we had as kids or how to create that kind of fun. Over the years, I've learned a few guidelines.

For one, it helps to *do something different* from the usual routine every once in a while. A little bit of change every now and then can make life seem lighter and more fun. How else to explain PB&Js in bed on Friday nights? It wasn't a *rule* that you had to brush your teeth before going to bed, but it *was* the routine. And eating food after that *was not* the routine, which is probably what made Friday night PB&Js more fun.

Anticipation helps, too. *Anticipation builds excitement* and adds to a sense of fun. It was fun to look forward to a new activity every night after dinner and wonder what it might be. Capture the Flag, a Camper-Counselor hunt, a baseball game, Skit Night? A regularly scheduled special day or night of the week with a surprise activity can go a long way toward encouraging good behavior and fostering joy.

Resisting the impulse to criticize is an important part of creating an environment that fosters success and joy, and keeps life fun. As adults, we feel responsible for making sure the young people in our lives don't do things that will hinder their success in the future. But even though we are well intentioned, we often let criticism take the place of encouragement and instruction. At Flying Eagle, we encouraged effort and, importantly, did not criticize defeat. When criticism is withheld, effort encouraged and achievement celebrated, the joy of trying something new can blossom. Guided by our philosophy and vision, we nurtured and supported the efforts of young boys to try new things even when the effort didn't go well. The end result was never valued more than the boy, and that helped keep the effort fun.

Singing silly songs is always fun. Song Night brought a chance to be creatively juvenile and rewarded for it. Each cabin was responsible for making up a song, usually to a well-known tune. Chris, a camper from 1976–80 told us, "Whenever one of those songs comes on the radio, I start singing it with campers' words. My kids think I've gone crazy!"

Then there were the **harmless pranks**. When you put boys together for any length of time, you can be sure they will become creative in their pursuit of fun. There are just not enough activities in a day to exhaust the creative energy of adolescent boys, and we tolerated pranks that were not harmful or mean.

Camper pranks that got the most attention were tent raids. Once the night counselor on duty had left the tent after the boys seemed to be asleep, the campers would sneak out of their tent, go to another tent, do something outrageous and sneak back without being caught. The "something outrageous" might be soaking the other campers with squirt guns or taking something—a towel or underwear—and waiting for it to be missed. Once missed, they would return it openly, or quietly in another tent raid to demonstrate their ability to sneak around the other tent.

Of course, they were often caught, if not by the on-duty counselor, then by Alex, who liked to roam the camp grounds at night, checking to make sure all was well. If it were a quiet little raid, with no harm done, the raiders would be shooed back to bed. But if it created an uproar that woke other campers, it meant the offenders would have to run laps around the ball field. Or worse, suffer the loss of Candy Store.

In the summer of 1971, the Eagles, our oldest camper group, were creative. Jeff, in his sixth year as a camper, told the story:

> *The Eagles come up with a plan to ring the bell at midnight. We vote for George to do it, but he is hesitant. He fears he will lose his Candy Store if he is caught. He becomes more receptive when everyone in the group agrees to give him our Candy Store for the entire session. He is finally convinced when we tell him that Merrill is on tent duty and everyone knows that Merrill can't catch anybody. The deed is done, and camp history is made. But George is nailed in the process.*

The next morning, George faces Alex prepared to lose his
Candy Store, but confident in the knowledge that he will
get all of ours. But Alex correctly surmises that George did
not come up with this plan by himself and takes Candy
Store away from all the Eagles for the whole session!

Matching wits with campers, or even secretly helping, was a hot topic for counselors. Dave remembers "the nights spent in dark sweat suits on tent duty just waiting for the Apaches to try to make a tent raid." Norm said one of his best memories was "trying to figure out what prank I could let the Eagles get away with at the end of each session. I think the best was the year they planted a tree in the middle of the ball field and moved all their bunks underneath it on the last night."

It wasn't just campers who engineered pranks. The counselors did, too. Dave remembers creating "swamp monster feet that we left tracks of all over camp to prove that the monster stories were true." Our son Paul did his share by carving deer feet and making tracks that seemed to walk right up to the tent door flaps. He also put together a shiny, silver, flashing UFO that on dark nights he sent through the trees with a pulley.

One of the longest running pranks involved the Counselor's Quarters or CQ. How it started, I'll never know. In 1960, believing the counselors needed a place to rest while off-duty, we put up a building that was part craft shop and part private quarters for the counselors. In 1972, when a new craft shop went up, the counselors had the old building to themselves. Not long after that, campers began to hear bowling pins clanging in the CQ. Paul had gone to a bowling alley and recorded the sound of falling pins. The counselors liked to play it when campers walked by.

The campers decided there must be a basement under the CQ that housed a bowling alley, and the legend was that you had to move a Lazy-Boy chair to access a secret door that led to the basement. The counselors never said there was a bowling alley, but they never said there wasn't. Year after year, the story grew. Counselors brought bowling balls to camp and walked around with them. Even now, years after camp has ended, camper alumni who come back to visit still ask for a chance to visit the bowling alley.

A few years after the bowling alley was installed, the counselors said they'd added a pizza machine in the basement. The campers were convinced, possibly because the counselors were not above walking out of the CQ eating pizza. At least once, and probably more often, when a cabin group won pizza as a prize, a pizza made in the kitchen was sneaked through the woods and delivered from the CQ. Curtis wrote, "I'd still love to see that pizza machine and that bowling alley!"

After reading other camper memories on the Camp Flying Eagle website, Arnie added,

> *Reading the other memories certainly gave me goosebumps. What a great feeling to rush back to being 11 years old and all the fun we had. I loved the Color Wars, the baseball games, swimming the lake, long overnight bike rides, boxing matches with the giant gloves, shooting .22 rifles. Wow. We certainly had too much fun. Now that I have kids of my own, I am concerned about being able to find them experiences like we had.*

Creating fun doesn't have to be complicated. In fact, building fun into your everyday routine is easier than you think. By allowing some creativity and building anticipation, even everyday happenings can become fun events.

At Camp Flying Eagle, it was part of our routine. Sleeping in on Sundays, bedtime stories every night, Movie Night in pajamas with popcorn, Kool-Aid and cookies every afternoon at 3:00, playing bingo when it rained, five dollars to spend any way you wanted on Mackinac Island, candy bars and more candy bars....

Too much fun? No. Just about right.

> "The more you are here, the more *fun* it is!"
>
> **Keith**

REMEMBER...

Let your heart be light and everything else will improve. In *The 7 Habits of Highly Effective People,* Stephen Covey writes that the seventh habit, sharpening the saw, should come first. In other words, taking time to sharpen the saw before you start cutting wood will save time and make everything easier. Building in fun is like sharpening the saw. The results you hope for will be much easier to achieve.

CHAPTER TEN

— ACTION STEPS —

1. Every family's life has a "rhythm" to it, a routine, whether you have planned it or not. Think about your own family routine or rhythm. What can you do to interrupt it with something "fun"?

2. Pick a regularly scheduled night each week, or even once a month, for a surprise activity. Your goal is to build anticipation and excitement.

3. Have a family song contest and come up with a song to sing on the way to buy groceries or on the way to school. Debbie told me that when she was working and taking her sons, Brian and Scott, to preschool every morning, she bundled them in matching "Top Gun" bomber jackets and played "*Highway To The Danger Zone*" every day at top volume as they pulled into the preschool parking lot.

4. Resist criticism! Everything for young children is a learning experience. Even if you have to repeat yourself, repeat calmly—over and over. Teach calmly. Instruct calmly. Demonstrate calmly.

5. A word about "pranks." These can backfire and take all of the fun out of life instead of adding to it. Generally speaking, pranks and practical jokes *by* adults *that target a specific kid* are *not* fun. No prank or practical joke should ever embarrass, undermine, or make fun of a child. The internet is full of videos of parents carrying out pranks that leave a child in tears while the adults laugh uproariously. Think carefully about the message your son may absorb. It will repeat throughout life.

I was eight years old my first year, so this would have been 1973. I then came to camp every year through 1979. I stayed for the full 7 weeks. To this day, I have wonderful memories of that time. It made a very positive impact on my life. I really loved the water skiing, but also all the cookouts and overnight outings, 40 Pines, biking trips, the Manistee canoe trips. I remember the guys that stayed for both sessions always got to go on a unique trip in-between sessions. I remember being buddies with all the guys from Mexico, since most of them also stayed the whole summer. So many fun things."

Jack

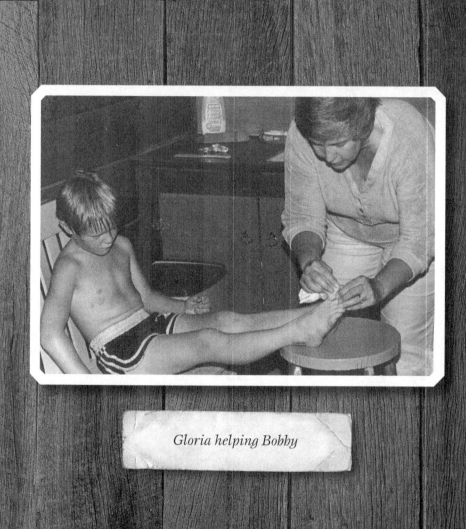

Gloria helping Bobby

CHAPTER ELEVEN

THE ONE THING
THAT LASTS

All children need to feel loved and cared for wherever they are, whether at home, at camp or in school. To them, it is validation that "people like me" and "I'm OK." Even with all of the great activities and fun, the primary reason for our success at Flying Eagle may have been our real affection for the boys. Alex, Dick, Gloria and I knew all of the campers. We consciously took on the role of surrogate parents and grandparents, bestowing love, caring and guidance on them. In turn, we encouraged them to care for themselves, each other, the camp, the land and the nature and beauty that surrounds us all.

No matter what role we play, we all have opportunities to share love and caring with the children around us. When I was young, we lived next door to my grandparents, who cared for my sister and me while my parents worked. I deeply remember the love and caring they bestowed upon my sister and me.

At camp, I saw many other examples of the difference a grandparent's caring can make. I delivered the mail to the KBs. One summer, for six days every week, I delivered the *Milwaukee Journal* to one of them. It was a gift from his grandfather, who understood how interested his grandson was in current events. Many years later, I was thrilled to see this same former KB on television as a political consultant to a presidential candidate. I would not be surprised to learn there were other ways his grandfather helped him find his path in life. Grandparents can have a tremendous impact on grandchildren.

I heard a lot more about that when I served on a committee searching for candidates for the AARP National Board of Directors. I asked candidates, "Is there a phrase or song or poem that has served as a guide throughout your life?" So many mentioned a grandparent. One said, "It was my grandfather who told me, 'You'll always find differences in life. Look for the similarities.'" Another said, "When I was a boy, my grandfather said to me, 'You have a proud name. Never do anything to blemish it.'" A third said her grandfather told her, "'There's always a solution.' And I have always looked for one," she added.

One of the unique and special things about love and caring is that it multiplies. The caring that campers and counselors experienced at Flying Eagle, and that they said shaped their lives, gave them the desire to share it with others. Tom and Kate told us,

> *The "teaching experiences" we had as counselors paved the way for our careers as educators. The incredible positive atmosphere of helping to create successes for young people at CFE carried over into our combined 61 + years in the classroom.*

Merrill, our nature counselor, said, "As a result of working at Camp Flying Eagle, I became a teacher. I became the president of the Detroit Metropolitan Area Physics Teachers and then a Physics Teacher Resource Agent for the American Association of Physics

Teachers. Lots of really great stuff has happened as a result of my teaching that never would have happened if Alex hadn't hired me."

Campers told us that throughout life, they have taken with them the sense of oneness with nature and love for the land they learned from their camp experience: "Rolling up the tent flaps during rest period and listening to the wind rustling the leaves"… "Throwing down our sleeping bags and sleeping under the stars"… "Camping out on the ball field and watching the Northern Lights." Their love for the land multiplied as they shared it.

I've been amazed at how many campers have brought their families back to the Crooked Lake area to spend time in the summer. Dave, our waterfront director, told us, "I bought property near camp, have taken my son's Boy Scout troop down the same stretch of the Manistee and we've camped at the same camp sites. My kids can still hear me call them in off of the lake like I called in campers, even if they are at the other end." A group of campers went in search of a lake like Crooked Lake. They found one in Canada where they now own property and have summer reunions.

Many years after camp ended, I received an email from a camper with the sad news that his mother had died. "By the grace of God, we all got to tell her we loved her the night before she passed," he wrote. "One of the many things I learned from this tragedy is to tell those you love that you love them. You are one. I have told you many times that you and Alex have influenced my life, and I must tell you again. You are a role model, a mentor from the age of seven and a huge positive influence in my life. I know that many people have told you 'Thank you,' but I wanted to tell you again. My mother's influence and impact in my life can't be matched, but you and Alex are a close second."

This year Dick received a note about something that happened fifty years ago: "Coach, I have a letter you wrote my parents dated

June 6, 1967, about my play on the varsity baseball team that spring. It is the best compliment I have ever received, and you are the best baseball coach I have ever played for. God bless you, and thank you!"

It is gratifying to know that the bonds we create by our caring live on and on, adding security and strength to those we've loved throughout life. Take time to show the children around you that you care. So many children are missing that love and affection. If you are a teacher, you have a unique opportunity to leave a legacy greater than money can buy. You may be the one to show a child true caring for the first time.

One story about his life that Alex did share was of when he first came to the University of Michigan. He was unprepared, he said, for the academic rigor and ended up with a failing grade in his freshman English course. A failure would have meant the end of his scholarship, his diving, his college education and his future. He had nothing and no one to fall back on and was looking at the end of his dream. On a wing and a prayer he went to his professor to ask for a second chance. She believed in him. She changed his failing grade to a passing one to give him that second chance. He *never, ever* forgot her and her act of kindness. Every Christmas season until the day she died, he sent her a card to let her know she was remembered and appreciated.

Another example came to Alex from a former student, many years after he had left teaching:

Dear Mr. Canja,

You may not remember me, but I was one of the students who worked on the school paper in Ypsilanti when you were our counselor. One day you were so proud of the work we did that you took us all out to the Malt Shoppe for ice cream. We sat down, and the waitress came and took our order. Then she stood there. She just stood there until you told her to get on with it. We wanted ice cream! Finally, she left and brought us our sundaes and sodas.

Perhaps you didn't know it, but maybe you did. Black kids like me could buy ice cream at the Malt Shoppe, but we couldn't sit down inside to eat it. I went home and told my parents that I had integrated the Malt Shoppe!

You gave me the courage to do what I had to do in life. I became a high school counselor, and what I tried to do for my students is what you did for me—instill in them the courage they would need as they moved on with their lives.

That letter, written about an event that had taken place *forty-six years* earlier, just goes to show how much of an impact our actions can have.

Leave a legacy.

Love is the one thing that lasts.

REMEMBER...

Sometimes we think that children know how we feel about them because of how hard we work to provide them with food, shelter and opportunities. But they don't. You'll need to show them in ways that are personal to them. And you have to tell them. Your goal is to instill in your child a deep conviction that he is loved.

CHAPTER ELEVEN

ACTION STEPS

1. One of the best ways to show a child he is loved is to spend time with him. Find time to make him a priority by scheduling regular time to spend together each week *doing something he enjoys.* This is not always easy. Playing his favorite video game with him, watching the same movie for the 16th time, or recreating Jurassic Park with plastic dinosaurs might not be your first choice of how to spend an hour or two, but it will be an investment with a powerful payoff!

2. Listen to him. Keep in mind the truism that "students don't care how much you know until they know how much you care." Before you share your wisdom, listen to his.

3. There are many books with great suggestions on creative ways to tell your child you love him. For more ideas, visit *www.TheFlyingEagleFormula.com/toolbox.*

Terry Black and I attended Aquinas College together in the mid '70s. It was spring, 1975. I had just graduated and was looking for something to occupy my summer and provide a little cash before starting grad school in the fall. Terry told me his dad worked at some summer camp "Up North" and they had an opening for an assistant waterfront director. He told me I would love it. I had never seen a summer camp before, but I had worked as a lifeguard and my Red Cross card was still current. I figured I had nothing to lose so I phoned this guy, Alex, who hired me based on Terry's recommendation.

Two weeks later, I found myself stranded in the middle of nowhere. My '64 Mercury had snapped a U-joint. I was expected at camp that day to help get things ready, and I hadn't thought to bring phone numbers so I couldn't even call. And so, the Mercury became my abode for the night until it could be fixed. The next day, a sheepish, unkempt, unshaven, six-foot-four mop-head pulled into camp feeling guilty and wondering if he still had a job.

The first person I met was Mrs. Black, who immediately gave me a big hug. I am convinced she believed she had just discovered her long-lost son because that is exactly how she treated me and still does to this day. Of course, Mr. Black, Alex and Tess adopted me, too. The other counselors became like brothers. The rest, as they say, is history.

My career at Camp Flying Eagle lasted all of ten weeks: seventy days. But what days! What nights! What a summer! Those moments…those memories…of fun times and outstanding people. They are tucked away deep in my heart…not so deep that I can't take them out and hold them when my soul needs refreshing. They will be with me always.

Mike, Assistant Waterfront Director, 1975

PART TWO

LESSONS *of* SUCCESS

Winter on Crooked Lake

CHAPTER TWELVE

THE MOST IMPORTANT LESSON

In 1983, Alex and I made the difficult decision to close our beloved camp. On the last day of our last session, we said our last good-bye to our last camper and stood there in the quiet, lost in the reality of it all and the depth of our private thoughts.

Along with closing the camp, we were also retiring. My father had recently died, and my mother was living alone in Florida with Parkinson's disease. She needed me. I decided to retire from my job as the director of Michigan's Area Agencies on Aging Association. Alex was retiring from his job as administrative assistant and right hand to five, successive state superintendents of Michigan's public schools.

We moved to Florida, but continued to spend our summers on Crooked Lake in a beautiful log cabin across from the camp. Many years ago, we'd bought it from one of the original settlers who had built it by hand in the 1940s, including its massive fieldstone fireplace with split rocks of granite and quartz that sparkle in the lamplight. Next to the former camp property and across the lake from our cabin, are Dick and Gloria, in the cottage they built and lived in while we ran the camp together. We eventually sold the camp property to the grandson of a lake neighbor and were later able to watch and smile as their kids swam the lake or paddled about in boats. For nearly twenty summers after the camp closed, we relaxed and enjoyed the woods and the lake, the company of Dick and Gloria and the quiet of the trees.

It was the summer of 2002 when Alex began to complain of pain in his back. As a swimmer and diver, he had learned to live with aches and pains and he was never the type to complain about anything. But this was different. We headed for the local family practice office. When the doctor sent Alex down the hall for X-rays he pulled me aside. "When older men come to see me with back aches," he said, "I check out the possibility of prostate cancer." Prostate cancer? I had never given a thought to prostate cancer. I didn't even know much about it. But the doctor was right, and it had spread.

I don't think I realized the seriousness of what we were facing, of what I might be facing, but looking back, I can see that Alex had a much greater understanding. Before we left the cottage for the summer, he took Debbie and me on a tour and gave us detailed instructions on how to close it down for the winter and open it up for the summer, what to do with the car and boat batteries and where we could find the tools for different tasks, just in case. When we got back to Florida he took me to buy a new car. Our old car was fine, but he insisted it was time to get a new one, just in case.

I had been planning to surprise Alex with a book of memories for the fiftieth anniversary of our purchase of Flying Eagle, but that was still three years away. Now I wasn't exactly sure how many years we would still have together, so I wrote to our former campers and counselors and asked them, "Do you have memories you could share now?"

The response was overwhelming, and the replies beautiful and touching. It was then we truly learned of the long-lasting impact that our love and caring has on others. We learned that no effort is too small or ever wasted. That is when we realized, with great joy, that the thoughts and memories we sought to create of success and achievement, of belonging and caring, really had repeated themselves throughout the lives of our campers and had created more: more achievement, more success, more belonging and caring. Former campers and counselors gave credit to the summers spent at Flying Eagle for their values, their professions and the direction of their lives. We learned our efforts brought lasting joy.

Hector (1977–1983) wrote:

The best years of my life were at CFE. I remember how sad I spent the first summer after Camp Flying Eagle was closed. That same feeling knocks on my door of my heart every summer.

Frank (1977–1983) told us:

I realized how much CFE meant to me the other day when I was able to recite an entire day's schedule to my son, Peter. I have actually found myself waking him up in the morning very similar to how Mr. Black and Alex used to wake us up: 'All right! All right! All right! Everybody up! It's a great day at Flying Eagle!'

Ross (1972–1974) shared this:

I have talked so much about Flying Eagle that when my son was ten he asked me if he could go to CFE. It broke my heart to tell him that camp was no longer in business.

CFE—a camp where a boy could be a boy and learn lessons that later in life would help him to be a man.

Some memories were funny. The camp was on a septic tank system and with seventy boys and counselors using six toilets in the dorm, Alex always had a few sturdy plungers ready.

Fred wrote:

> *I remember one time that some of us put too much toilet paper in the toilet. It backed up, and Alex got quite mad about it. He called us all together…told us all we needed to use was three sheets of toilet paper, not all at once, but one at a time. Alex, I'm sorry to say, I've tried to use only three sheets. But I have not been able to use less than nine, using two or three sheets at a time.*

He sent another story, too. I laughed so hard I cried when I read it. Fred said it actually happened. I hope no one calls me up to say it is really true.

> *We were making a trip in the camp bus from Camp Flying Eagle to camp out at Grand Marais. We stopped at a rest area/park next to the Cut River Bridge on Highway 2 in the UP. We were having great fun hauling rocks from the side of the bridge and then dropping them off the side of the bridge (not on cars!). Someone called us back to the rest area. I thought we were in trouble because of dropping rocks off of the bridge.*
>
> *But when we got back to the rest area, we were told that one of the campers was in the restroom/out house. He stuck his head down through the hole so he could peek through to the girls' side and fell in. He was so upset that he couldn't hold on to a rope so one of the counselors had to climb down to tie him to the rope so he could be pulled out.*

I'm not sure, but I seem to remember there was no water there to wash them off and the bottom of the Cut River was too far so they sat on the floor in the back of the bus until we got down near the lake. I don't know who the counselor was, but I still feel for him. I tell this story at my wastewater treatment plant meetings.

The synchronicity of some stories amazed us. One year during his college spring break, the Black's son, Terry, and his friend, Ray, drove Dick's yellow station wagon from Michigan to Ft. Lauderdale, Florida. One day, when Ray was alone and driving the car, he decided to stop and pick up a random hitchhiker.

"Where are you from?" the hitchhiker asked. "St. Clair Shores, Michigan," Ray said. Then the hitchhiker asked, "Do you know Dick Black?"

"DO I KNOW HIM?" exclaimed Ray in amazement. "THIS IS HIS CAR!"

That hitchhiker was Rob, a Flying Eagle camper of many years.

Then there was this from Tim:

Not only did we wear our Flying Eagle T-shirts under our tuxes at my wedding, I still have carefully put away two CFE shirts. I also have very carefully put away my sashes from my six years at CFE, along with trophies for soccer, fishing and Camper of the Year.

These stories and many others brought peace to Alex as he reflected on our lives. Unfortunately, we didn't have years to enjoy them, only months. By June of 2003, he was too weak to make the trip back to the cottage in Michigan. Now in hospice care in our home, he lay on a hospital bed in the family room next to a couch where I could sit or sleep to be near him.

Bill, our former camper with orange hair and now an American Airlines pilot, called from Chicago. "I'm flying in," he said. He arrived the very next afternoon with a box. I brought him to where Alex lay, mostly unresponsive. Bill was undeterred. He carefully placed the box on the couch, opened it, reached in and held up, so Alex could see, all he had saved ever since he was ten years old: his award sashes from each of his five years as a camper, the trophies he had earned and pictures, T-shirts and other mementoes. As he showed each one, he shared special memories that had shaped his life.

Alex rallied as Bill talked, able to recognize him and even respond. Bill's visit and the many testimonials and memories that came from campers and counselors were the greatest gift he could have received. They showed him that his life had meaning and that he had made a difference in the lives of so many. That night, after Bill left and I finally fell asleep, Alex slipped away.

In our quest to do the right thing in our lives, for ourselves, our children and others, we pursue goals, we strive for recognition and we try to shape ourselves, our children and the world around us. After he was diagnosed with cancer and realized his adventure here might soon be ending, Alex looked back on all that striving and shook his head. "Old too soon, wise too late," he said. Real meaning comes from something else. He wrote about that something else one day when we were attending a program on expanding mental horizons. They wanted us to try our hand at poetry. Alex's poem ended with that something else, the most important thing he had come to understand and that so many had shared with him at the end: "I was loved."

Gathering once again at the Council Fire to celebrate

CHAPTER THIRTEEN

THE
REUNION

In 2006, the fiftieth anniversary of our purchase of Flying Eagle and twenty-three years after the camp closed, we held a reunion. It started with a phone call. "Gordon and I have been talking," said Bill, "and we have decided that we need a camp reunion."

It took a year of searching, but we finally pieced together a list of names and addresses of former campers and counselors and sent out invitations. Then we held weekend work parties on the former camp property, raking, painting, clearing, nailing. Campers and counselors came to help as we turned the clock back twenty-three years.

We held the reunion on Alex's birthday, August 11, 2006, a beautiful, sunny, incredible day, joined by over 100 campers, counselors and family members. We followed the camp schedule, did camp activities, had a camp cookout and, because it was his birthday, ate banana splits.

At the end, we held a Council Fire. Dick rang the bell and campers, now in their thirties, forties, fifties and sixties, lined up in front of the Chow Hall, as they had so long ago. Among them were doctors, lawyers, teachers, bankers, business owners and executives, computer specialists and one airline pilot. Counselors, in their fifties and sixties and seventies, walked across the baseball field and took their places along the Council Fire path, their arms crossed as in days gone by.

It touched me when I saw so many men putting on their sashes, still full of the awards they had earned as boys. Sashes that once hung loosely when they were eight- or nine-year-old boys now hugged their chests and stretched tightly from their right shoulder to just under their left arm, but they wore them proudly as they marched to the Council Fire. Some young sons wore their dads' sashes. It touched my heart to realize how treasured those sashes were. They held memories of accomplishment and success, of goal-setting, initiative and the courage to try new things. Even though tucked away in boxes, drawers and maybe even old footlockers, they continued to remind the men, "You did it before, you can do it again." They are constant reminders of success.

It also showed me something else. Even though we weren't there every step of the way in the lives of our campers, our actions had a lasting impact. The boys came to camp for only a few short weeks in the summer. A handful of boys stayed for the full season of seven weeks, but the rest were with us for only a three- or four-week session. That's it. While some came back year after year, for five, six, seven or more years, most returned for far fewer. If you think about it, a typical camper spent only four months of his entire life at Camp Flying Eagle. Yet, that short period of time had a lasting, positive impact. I find this so very encouraging. It means it is truly worth our time to make the effort to make a difference, no matter how short the time we have.

On that day in August, we lit the Council Fire and gave out awards, including gold felt Service stars to the young sons of campers who worked alongside their dads on weekends preparing for the reunion. We sang camp songs, yelled camp yells, counted echoes and softly sang taps. Then one by one, the campers and their families quietly left in single file, walking in silence down the Council Fire path. Silent until the moment the toes of their shoes touched the outermost edge of center field.

Then, as Alex would say, all hell broke loose, and everyone ran, screaming and yelling across the ball field.

Within every boy lies magic that leads to success

CHAPTER FOURTEEN

MAKE A DIFFERENCE

We all, in some way, wish we were better than we are, don't we? We want the same for our children. But neither Alex nor I was or is perfect, and I have learned this lesson: you don't have to be perfect to make a profound and positive difference in the life of a child. You can make mistakes. You can judge yourself harshly and believe that others are just as harsh in their judgment of you. Even so, as imperfect as you may be, you can still be the one who changes another's life for the better.

The most important ingredients are not that you be perfect, or that you get it "right," or that you do it the way we did, or that you have a supportive partner, or a perfect one or even one at all. What does matter is that you give the young people in your life experiences that will build long-lasting memories of success; that you let them make decisions and give them opportunities to be responsible; that you reward their accomplishments with your recognition; and perhaps most important, when they make mistakes, as we all do, that you not be as hard on them as you are on yourself. Take time to listen to them, respect their opinions and let them make their own choices about personal matters. Encourage new experiences, have fun with them and show your love and caring. Perfection is not a requirement.

Alex was committed to bringing magic into young lives and to giving young boys the building blocks for success. Mitch, who owned a successful Which Wich sandwich franchise in Petoskey, told us:

> *I have so many great memories of CFE...memories that shaped the values of who I became. Among my favorites: Sitting on the porch and talking to everyone about nothing. Fishing with Jeff before anyone else was awake. Many great trips to Mackinac Island. Bingo on rainy nights in the Rec Hall. PB&Js after Council Fire. Ice cream at Dairy Queen in Mancelona. Sneaking up on Paul to listen to him play the piano. Cereal box candles and lanyard key chains. Green Chapel and Sunday breakfast buffet. Spending the summer of 1980 in the Boat House as a KB. CFE did a lot of great things for me—a life-altering, positive influence.*

In 2003, two former campers who had been together at Flying Eagle for five summers and became lifelong friends, returned to visit. Hector later wrote:

> *That was like a rebirth for me. In the summer of 1983, I left a part of me in the woods and at the bottom of the lake. I just wasn't ready to say good-bye, and so I said 'See you next year.' But twenty years went by before I could be reunited with the little kid who learned to live life at Camp Flying Eagle.*

At our 2006 reunion, one counselor, now retired after thirty years in the classroom, looked around and said, "I can't believe how many of us went into teaching."

Bill, in addition to encouraging us to hold the fiftieth anniversary reunion, started an Alex Canja Scholarship Fund at the University of Michigan. The scholarship supports young athletes who want to go into teaching. Bill said he did it because, in his words:

> *It is worth repeating what Alex has done for me in my life. Virtues like persistence, fitness, patience, a love for the out-of-doors, a love for your fellow man will guide me for the rest of my life. You can't learn that from a book. You have to live it to have it sink in.*

None of us is perfect, but each of us has the ability to give love, caring and respect to others. When you pair that with choice, achievement, recognition and a little bit of fun in the life of a young child, you create the positive memories and positive beliefs that will continue to attract more of the same in the future. Then, the magic can and will happen.

CHAPTER FIFTEEN

THE TOOLBOX

All men in Michigan's North Country have a personal toolbox, or sometimes even a garage, filled with hammers, screwdrivers, files, pliers and an assortment of special tools and gadgets that come in handy when needed. They are a prized collection of resources that can turn any guy into a MacGyver hero, prepared and ready to save the day. During the time we ran camp, Alex had a whole building. The "Utility Building" was a dedicated space for storing coffee cans full of nails and screws, odd parts of windows, doors, unknown machines, screwdrivers and ratchet wrenches of ALL sizes. He also had a portable toolbox just the right size for carrying around to fix things.

One day, I needed to take Alex's small pickup truck somewhere, so I got into the driver's seat and drove away. I didn't realize that the tailgate was down with Alex's toolbox perched on the edge. Of course, it fell off somewhere along the way. Alex immediately knew what had happened and was REALLY unhappy.

Frantically, I retraced my steps back and forth over the entire route, but no toolbox. I went to the hardware store and bought some more tools, but of course, because they weren't his old tools, they didn't make him any happier. Finally, I put an ad in the local paper.

Unbelievably, a woman called to say she had found Alex's toolbox along the road and, knowing how important a toolbox is to any Up North man, had been searching for the owner ever since.

In this story of Camp Flying Eagle, we've shared with you another kind of toolbox. At the start of this book you'll find the quotation from Napoleon Hill, "What the mind of man can conceive and believe, the mind of man can achieve." The vision you create of the end result you hope to see of your parenting or of your teaching is your effort to conceive and believe what's possible. You can think of it as the foundation and frame of a house you and your child will build together, a house of the future. We also like to think of that vision as a unique toolbox, designed to hold customized tools to help you in your adventure of raising young people to a life of success.

We've shared with you the best tools to put into your toolbox:

- ➤ forming a mental picture of the outcome you are trying to create,
- ➤ finding ways to celebrate a child's strengths and accomplishments,
- ➤ finding the "something" at which a child can succeed,
- ➤ not criticizing less-than-perfect efforts,
- ➤ finding a way for a child to contribute as part of a team,
- ➤ building traditions, even from everyday activities,
- ➤ creating and keeping a schedule and routine,
- ➤ giving a child advance notice of the schedule and time to transition,

- allowing a child to have personal choice over personal matters,

- holding rules to a minimum and only about the most important things,

- taking time to *really* listen to a child's ideas and opinions,

- exploring new places,

- building anticipation and fun into every week—even every day,

- making sure boys aren't hungry if you want them to pay attention,

- sharing genuine love and caring, and

- not being as hard on a child as you are on yourself.

The Camp Flying Eagle program was designed to embed a pattern of success in young minds, knowing that patterns created in childhood repeat themselves throughout our lives. The experience of success, the memory of success and the emotion of success all change our way of thinking. Having experienced it once, our thoughts turn to its re-creation, to doing it again, to re-experiencing the thoughts and emotions that fill us when we succeed. By helping children experience success, we help them create a mental pattern of success.

This is the real secret of success—that we attract what we think about. Good or bad, when you type a thought into the Google search bar of your mind, it will bring you more of the same. Good or bad. That means you'll want to start now to envision the future you want to see and not the past you didn't like. And then carry that positive vision to the children around you.

The following resources are other tools we want to share. Many of these resources we have tried ourselves, some have been recommended by friends or former campers and counselors, and still others are links to more information. You can find updated links and any additional information we've added at *www.TheFlyingEagleFormula.com/toolbox.*

Summer Camp Information

American Camp Association: *www.acacamps.org* Search over 2,400 ACA Accredited camps.

www.Bridges4Kids.org/summercamp A list of camps providing programs for children with special needs.

Michigan Summer Camps

Mystic Lake YMCA Camp: *www.mysticlakecamp.com*
High quality camping programs for children and teens. "Our programs focus on helping campers develop the skills that are necessary for them to have great success in life. We believe our programs help children gain confidence, make great friends, teach lifelong skills and further their maturity. All of our programs place a strong emphasis on skill building, teambuilding and personal growth. Whether your child registers for our traditional Mystic Experience program (ages 7-14) or opts for one of our many specialty camps, (such as Fishing, Horseback Riding, Teen Adventure, etc.), we believe you will find comfort in knowing they are safe and having fun!"

Camp Tanuga: *www.camptanuga.com*
"Tanuga is deeply committed to the philosophy of a traditional camping experience. Values, as depicted by our respect for nature, the environment, and the development of accepting others for who they are, stand out in our mission. Our objective for each camper is to build self-confidence, develop a cohesive family feeling and create the assurance of belonging. The sense of accomplishment and confidence that develop each summer carry over throughout the year into the campers' classrooms, future relationships, and during periods of difficult transitions into adulthood."

Camp Lookout: *www.lookoutsummer.com*
"Our camp is small enough for everyone to know each other, yet large enough to offer diversified and interesting programs. Campers

and staff plan daily activities together and share the responsibility for establishing many of the necessary policies and rules of the camp. This community of campers and staff share the necessary camp chores—assisting with meal preparation, washing dishes, cleaning cabins and helping with simple construction projects. Campers choose their activities two times each day and most activities are offered to every camper regardless of age, gender or cabin group. We attempt to make choices as varied as possible."

Crystalaire Adventures: *www.crystalaireadventures.com*
"Today, the focus on non-competitive learning environments, the freedom to choose your daily journeys, and opportunities for participants to discover friends, themselves, and the world around them endures with adaptive programming strategies to meet the needs of kids in the 21st century. Crystalaire continues in the spirit of adventure-based alternative education, as it has for almost a century. Through boating, backpacking, biking and more, we help campers foster a sense of belonging to the rest of the world and gain the skills necessary to change strangers into friends. Our expeditions are built around community involvement: every trip participant is included in planning and preparation for the trip, deciding activities, leading discussions and carrying out the daily work of out-of-door living. Wherever possible, this includes decision making about routes and directions, meals and more."

Camp Walden: *www.campwaldenmi.com*
"Founded in 1959, Walden is a coed overnight camp for campers entering 2nd grade through 11th grade. We're in the Northern Michigan's Lower Peninsula on a pristine 150 acres outside the city of Cheboygan. Walden stretches along Long Lake, a clear, spring-fed body of water, and camp's terrain ranges from lush meadows to old-growth forests. As a family-owned, traditional summer camp, we offer a *diverse range of activities* from land and water sports to horseback riding; from rockets and radio to the visual and

performing arts. Walden campers roast marshmallows, sing silly songs, star-gaze and drink "bug juice"! And they also do less-traditional camp stuff, like mountain biking, gardening and yoga. Kids choose their own activity program and, with the *guidance of a fun, committed and highly professional staff,* find out what it's like to be "on their own" for part of the summer."

YMCA Hayo-Went-Ha: *www.hayowentha.org*
"Camp Hayo-Went-Ha has 110 years of tradition and experience to provide incredible adventures campers remember for a lifetime. Our camp motto, Each for All...All for Each is evident in all we do. Boys learn to work together, to support each other and to respect what each member of the cabin has to offer. The wonderful variety of camp trips reinforce the value of teamwork all the while learning to appreciate the beauty that surrounds you. We also offer Challenge Programs. Campers can climb a 50-foot tower with six routes, a 36-foot high ropes course, and a 28-foot pamper pole along with a freestanding zip line and team vertical elements. Discover SCUBA lessons are available for every camper."

Resources That Explore How Our Thoughts and Emotions Create Our Present and Future

The Nature of Personal Reality: A Seth Book by Jane Roberts. Get started at *http://sethquotes.paradisenow.net/seth_excerpts_part_i.html*

www.TheWork.com: Sometimes as adults we are not as positive and helpful as we might be with the children around us. Often we react to things in our own past with beliefs that really don't fit the situation. Here is an easy, free and amazingly effective way to uncover and examine those beliefs. On the website, look for the link to "Resources." Open or download the "Judge Your Neighbor" worksheet and the "One Belief at a Time" worksheet. Fill in the name of a child or adult who is really driving you nuts and follow the simple directions. You can also watch videos of others going through the exercise.

The Bible: Regardless of which version one reads, the message of the Resurrection calls us to faith. The strong emphasis on family and caring for one another is the foundation of our desire to give our children the tools and experiences that will enrich their lives and lead to success.

A Course In Miracles: Christian in the terms used, but universal in its application, this treatise suggests that what we think creates the world we see and experience. It also includes 365 lessons to follow, one for each day of the year. We recommend the Circle of Atonement edition as it is the most complete and easy to understand.

The Silva Method: We first learned this method of accessing inner awareness in the 1970s from reading a book, but classes are also available. It works. "Enriching the planet by empowering the individual. A better you…A better world!" *www.silvamethodct.com*

Deliberate Receiving: by Melody Fletcher. A step-by-step approach that clearly explains *exactly* HOW to manifest the reality you wish to live in.

Transcending the Maya Matrix Using the Seven Simple Steps: Our Innate Guide to Co-Creation and Self-Realization: by Omar M. Makram. How to uncover the personal "GPS system" within you that leads to manifesting a life you love.

As a Man Thinketh: a classic by James Allen

Think and Grow Rich: the classic by Napoleon Hill.

The Power of Awareness: a classic by Neville Goddard.

A new generation

EPILOGUE

The year Debbie's first son, my first grandson, was born, was the last year Camp Flying Eagle operated as a summer camp. He and his younger brother never had a chance to become Little Eaglets, dormers, tenters, KBs or counselors. Even though they came to Crooked Lake each summer, ran around the buildings and swam in the lake, they kept asking if they could go to Camp Flying Eagle, too.

Seven years after the camp closed, Debbie and I came up with a surprise for them. We found some extra sashes, dug out award badges and devised a plan to give them a week of camp experience based on the Flying Eagle program and activities. Alex was the camp director and Debbie and I were the counselors.

One of the great things about "going to camp" is how different it is from being at home. We realized that one of the biggest differences is the schedule. So, even though the kids were technically "at home," we followed the camp schedule. We started after lunch on Sunday because that had always been the day and time for campers to arrive. That night we had Movie Night, just like at camp. The next morning at 7:00 a.m., Alex went through the house yelling,

"All Right, All Right, All Right! Everybody UP! It's a Great Day at Flying Eagle!"

The kids did cals, washed up and we rang first and second bell. They stood at attention and reported at Formation. They picked up their rooms for Inspection. They made crafts, collected leaves, rocks and bugs for their nature award and wrote stories for the camp newspaper. They slept outside for their overnight award, had a picnic for their cookout award and hiked to the store for their hiking award. Because we were at Crooked Lake, they all swam the lake for their swimming award and had a chance to try rowing and canoeing. In our camp program, six awards earned a green eagle.

They loved it! The next year Debbie signed them up for a week at Mystic Lake Camp, a camp run by the YMCA that offers a wide variety of activities. They loved Mystic Lake and happily went away to camp each summer for the next five years.

When Debbie became the executive director of an organization that helps parents of children with special needs, she heard from many parents who wanted their children to experience the fun of summer camp, but for one reason or another, their children could not attend. Either the camps did not offer enough support and supervision for different special needs or the camps that were available were already full or just too expensive.

When she later started a nonprofit organization, Bridges4Kids, as a way to help parents and professionals find help and support for *all* kids, she looked for a way to help more kids have a summer camp experience. As part of that, she began posting information on summer camps on the Bridges4Kids website. We've included the link in the Toolbox.

She also began to dream of a way to bring to all kids a summer camp experience that builds a foundation for success. That dream became "Summer Camp In A Box," a program that includes everything a parent, grandparent, or other caring adult needs to embed a success mindset in a week of "summer camp at home" based on the Flying Eagle Formula. A step-by-step, how-to kit for "camp counselors" will be included with instructions, a daily schedule, tips, hints and helps.

We believe in the summer camp experience and especially in the Flying Eagle Formula. We know that the secret to creating confident, secure and successful adults lies in the experiences they have as children and what those experiences teach them about themselves. The goal of Summer Camp In A Box is to give all children an opportunity to try new experiences and to create memories of success. Regardless of our abilities, Summer Camp In A Box is designed to help *every* child experience success, feel it, *know* it and remember it in a program filled with fun and joy.

If you know a child who would like to experience summer camp, and an adult who is willing to share a week to provide that experience, we'd like to share Summer Camp In A Box with you. You can learn more at *www.SummerCampInABox.com.*

May your Little Eaglets soar!
Tess

NEXT STEPS

So where do you go from here? What do you do next? If you've followed the Action Steps we've outlined in each chapter, you will probably have already tried a few new ideas. But if not, it's all about starting. You don't have to do it all and you don't have to do it all at once. You just need to start. Remember, perfection is not a requirement.

That's what we love so much about the things you've learned in this book. These are simple concepts that you can apply without too much effort, but the results from the ideas we've shared and the resources you can find in this book's toolbox, and in the online toolbox at *www.TheFlyingEagleFormula.com/toolbox,* will make a transformative difference in the life of a boy. In your life, too. It's the journey of a lifetime and this is the beginning.

Many people who read this book before it went to print wanted to know if we could provide them with additional support and advice. As they talked to us about implementing the ideas, we were able to identify some roadblocks that were keeping them from getting the results they wanted and to suggest some different techniques and resources that made a positive difference in their parenting and/or teaching journey and that will make a huge difference in a boy's future.

If that sounds like something you'd be interested in, something that could help along the way, visit *www.TheFlyingEagleFormula.com/toolbox* to get started.

And finally, thank you for reading and coming on this journey with us. We've poured our hearts into this project and if you've found it helpful and you bought this book on Amazon, please leave a review for us on Amazon. If you bought this book at one of our bookstore partners, please share comments at *www.Success4Kids.info*. Your comments will help others learwn about the benefits of the Flying Eagle Formula and your feedback helps us improve. Thank you!

Acknowledgments

This book would not have been possible without support and help from so many! We want to do our best to acknowledge our deep gratitude and love for all who encouraged us and kept us going through many years of working to share what we learned and believe is so important.

Thank You!...

To Bill Holmes, your support and belief in our mission, in Camp Flying Eagle, and in making this world a better place make us proud to know you and grateful to have your love. Thank you to both you and Wendy! We love you!

To Dick and Gloria Black, the Camp Flying Eagle experience that transformed so many lives just couldn't have happened without you. We love you more than words can say and cherish the summers we spend together on Crooked Lake.

To Brian and Scott Ehlers, Mom and Grandma love you! You are an inspiration to both of us and we couldn't be more proud of the fine young men you have turned out to be.

To Mitch, Merry and Max Brown, your unflagging friendship and our Saturday trips to Petoskey and your Which Wich sandwich shop sustained us through many years. Mitch, you were a great camper and KB and we are proud of your success!

To Sue, Greg and Nick Latta, Terry, Mary, Amy and Russell Black, Rick Black and Segio Black—you are like family and your love and support are cherished.

To Janie, Eddie, Fred, Joel, and Amber Crippen—we will never forget your parents, Ed and Cassie, and you are always welcome at Crooked Lake!

To Dave and Donna Pflum, Mike Pflum and Rose Pflum, the memory of Frank lives on. Free Period!

To Brad and Diane Smith and the seven Smith children (Nick, Claire, Bea, George, Francis, Henry and Chauncey) who took over Camp Flying Eagle after it closed and kept the memory alive, and the rest of the Smith family and Crooked Lake neighbors (Nick and Bonnie, Elizabeth and Fred, Stacia and Paul), thanks for being like family!

Thanks to Crooked Lake Neighbors who, for twenty-seven years, put up with guns going off all day at the rifle range, a motor boat circling the lake for two or three hours each day, a big, cast-iron bell that rang three big rings a minimum of seven times a day, and the yelling, screaming and laughter of sixty or more adolescent boys! We appreciate you!

To Jeff Walker and his Product Launch Formula and Launch Club team who have helped demystify how to share our important message and contribute to a better world. Thank You to coaches Donna Davis, Annette James, Don Crowther,

Marc Evans, and Jon Walker. A special thanks to Rose Etherington for keeping us all going forward.

To Michelle Lange of MLangeMedia, an awesome media company and Launch Club teammate, and David Hausen, thank you for your support, your ideas, and your willingness to travel to Michigan to capture professional video of the Camp Flying Eagle experience and testimonials from so many successful men!

To Jason Miller of Peaceful Media for your absolute enthusiastic support for Summer Camp in a Box! You helped us believe that the summer camp experience and success lessons really could be packaged and shared with a wide audience.

To Luis Carlos Flores (Ninosdeahora.tv) and Cecilia and Jason Hilkey (HappilyFamily.com) for setting a wonderful example of heartfelt and helpful parenting support.

To Ray Brehm of Dauntless, LLC and Mo Omar, who helped unravel the mysteries of book publishing!

To so many more PLF colleagues: Anyaa Lightheart, Jenna Lynsky, Tasha Nesbitt, Tom Garcia, Paul Beens, Gladys Clancy, Marie Pelton, Jeff Brewer, Melody Fletcher, Steve Pavlina, Daniel LeFave, Jason Friedman, Praveen Narra, Roy Davis Varner, Stephen Pollitt, Sajah Popham, Thembi Bheka, Julie Helmrich, Terrance Ward (and others we may have missed) for your help, support and especially comments you have shared along the way that helped keep us moving forward. You never know the ripple effects your comments and support can have.

To Tamara Dever and Monica Thomas of TLC Book Design for "getting it" and crafting a beautiful cover and inside design that helped convey our message.

To Kendra Lynn Perry, Becca Boyd Fedewa, Andrea Stay, Sophia Oswalt, Debbie Fuller, and Megan Tomazin Christensen (and her mom)—for the comments and suggestions you shared that helped make this book so much better!

And to the many, many campers and counselors we have met, loved and followed for so many years. We cannot possibly mention all of you, but a huge and heartfelt thank you to: Mitch Brown, Bill Holmes, Dave Steinbach, Hector Suarez Gomis, Jamie Magee, Merrill Falk, Rick and Terry Black, Bob, Tom, Dave and Jim Korroch, Jeff and Bryan Ehlers, Harvey, Steve, Clark and Brian Bell, Frank and Arnie Zuker, Chris Nugent, Jerry, Todd and Bob Hollister, Dar Mathews, Gordon Pennington, Tim Thieme, Hal Commerson, Mike Matthews, Terry Kauffman, Doug Wanty, Doug and Mike Dubin, Mike Sweeney, Bruce Tuttle, Dan Cunningham, John Polley, Ross Foner, Humberto Lopez-Mata, TJ McCullough, Mike Bielby, Benny Ibarra, Curtis Hawkins…and more.

Our blessings to all of you!

References

Allen, James. *As a Man Thinketh*. 1903.

Byrne, Rhonda. *The Secret*. Beyond Words Publishing. 2006.

Covey, Stephen. *7 Habits of Highly Successful People: Powerful Lessons in Personal Change*. Simon and Schuster. 1989.

Fletcher, Melody. *Deliberate Receiving: Finally the Universe Makes Some Freakin' Sense!* Hay House. 2015.

Franklin Covey Planners. Inspired by Benjamin Franklin who, at age 20, established a plan of 13 virtues for his life, which he wrote down and carried with him in a small book.

Goddard, Neville. *The Power of Awareness*. 1952. In early lectures and books, Goddard explored "The Law," the technique of visualization to manifest one's physical reality, and later "The Promise" to find one's true purpose.

Hill, Napoleon. *Think and Grow Rich*. Napoleon Hill Foundation. 1937.

Katie, Byron. *Loving What Is: Four Questions That Can Change Your Life*. Random House. 2002.

Kennedy, John F. 28th News Conference, March 21, 1962. "There is always inequity in life. Some men are killed in a war, and some men are wounded, and some men never leave the country, and some men are stationed in the Antarctic, and some are stationed in San Francisco. It's very hard in military or in personal life to assure complete equality. Life is unfair."

Makram, Omar M. *Transcending the Maya Matrix Using the Seven Simple Steps: Our Innate Guide to Co-Creation and Self-Realization*. CreateSpace. 2018.

Oliver, Bill. *Parent-to-Parent Drug Prevention Workshop*. PRIDE: National Parents Resource Institute for Drug Education. 1990.

Roberts, Jane. *The Nature of Personal Reality: A Seth Book*. Prentice-Hall. 1974.

Schucman, Helen. *A Course In Miracles: Complete & Annotated Edition*. Circle of Atonement. 2017.

Silva, Jose & Stone, Robert, PhD. *The Silva Mind Control Method for Getting Help From Your Other Side: Use Your Whole Mind for a New Dimension in Creative Power*. Pocket Books. 1989.

Tough, Paul. *How Children Succeed: Grit, Curiosity, and the Hidden Power of Character*. Houghton, Mifflin, Harcourt. 2012.

Vujicic, Nick. *Life Without Limits: Inspiration for a Ridiculously Good Life*. WaterBrook Press. 2010.

About the Authors

Tess Canja For 27 years, Tess created transformative summer camp experiences for thousands of young boys who went on to become successful husbands, fathers, businessmen and community leaders. At the same time she became a powerful advocate for older persons, first in Michigan as the Executive Director of Michigan's Area Agencies on Aging Association, then in Florida as Chair of the Committee to create a Florida Department of Elder Affairs, and finally, nationally as a member of the AARP Board of Directors and its national President. She has testified before Congress, met with Presidents and international leaders, and traveled across the United States to support community initiatives. Her life experiences give her a unique insight into the qualities that define success. It is her dream to create more happy and successful young men by sharing The Flying Eagle Formula. Now in her 90s, she continues to volunteer in her community as a member of her local AARP chapter. In her spare time she loves doing Sudoku puzzles and reading novels of intrigue, but her greatest joy is sharing time with grandsons Brian and Scott, reconnecting with Camp Flying Eagle campers and counselors, enjoying the beauty of Crooked Lake in the summer, and baking biscotti for family and friends.

Deb Canja is an attorney and success coach on a mission to help parents and others get information they need to help the children they love. She is the founder and CEO of Bridges4Kids, a national, non-profit organization providing online information for parents and professionals seeking help for kids from birth through college. She was the Executive Director of Michigan's Parent Training and Information Center teaching parents and schools successful ways to work together to help kids with disabilities and special needs. As a Michigan Assistant Attorney General and Deputy General Counsel, she protected the public by regulating insurance, lending, and mortgage services. Twice elected to her local community college Board of Trustees, she championed programs to make education affordable and accessible for all. Debbie was a "Little Eaglet" at Camp Flying Eagle until Tess and Alex "traded" kids with the owners of girls' camps who had sons. Later she became a camp counselor and taught waterskiing and crafts. Today she loves spending time with Tess, her two sons and a new grandson. Deb provides personal coaching for committed parents, teachers and coaches who want to take their parenting/mentoring to new levels of insight and effectiveness. *www.SuccessForKids.info*

Made in the USA
Middletown, DE
02 March 2020